VOLUME FOUR

HEARTS
AND
HANDS

CHRONICLES OF
THE AWAKENING CHURCH

HISTORY LIVES
VOLUME FOUR

HEARTS
AND HANDS

CHRONICLES OF
THE AWAKENING CHURCH

MINDY AND
BRANDON WITHROW

CF4•K

© Copyright 2007 Mindy and Brandon Withrow
Christian Focus Publications
ISBN: 978-1-84550-288-1
Reprinted 2009, 2011 and 2014

Published by Christian Focus Publications,
Geanies House, Fearn, Tain, Ross-shire,
IV20 1TW, Scotland, U.K.
www.christianfocus.com
email:info@christianfocus.com

Cover design by Jonathan Williams
Cover illustration by Jonathan Williams
Printed and bound by Nørhaven, Denmark

For Micaela, our fellow writer
and Elisabeth Grace, our future reader

May Jesus seal your hearts with
an inward sweet sense.

Contents

Awakening Church Timeline
1700-1860

1703	John Wesley and Jonathan Edwards born
1705	Sir Isaac Newton knighted by Queen Anne
1723	Johann Sebastian Bach becomes Cantor in Leipzig
1738	John Wesley converted at meeting on Aldersgate Street
1739	George Whitefield preaches at the Log College
1740	Gilbert Tennent preaches "The Danger of An Unconverted Ministry" sermon
1741	Jonathan Edwards preaches "Sinners in the Hands of an Angry God" sermon
1743	First performance of George Frideric Handel's *The Messiah*
1749	*Life of David Brainerd* published
1750	Johann Sebastian Bach dies
1758	American Presbyterians reunite after division over First Great Awakening
1770	James Hargreaves patents his spinning jenny
1773	John Newton writes "Amazing Grace;" Boston Tea Party
1776	American *Declaration of Independence* signed
1784	Methodist Episcopal Church formed
1789	Bastille stormed in France, igniting French Revolution
1792	William Carey founds Baptist Missionary Society
1793	Louis XVI executed
1794	Eli Whitney patents his cotton gin
1795	London Missionary Society formed
1797	Second Great Awakening begins
1802	First practical steamboat, *Charlotte Dundas*, launched in Scotland
1807	British Parliament passes *Abolition of Slave Trade Act*
1813	Elizabeth Fry first visits London's Newgate Prison

1814	Adoniram and Ann Judson leave for India and Burma; Francis Scott Key writes famed "The Star-Spangled Banner"
1815	Battle of Waterloo
1817	American Sunday School Union formed
1823	Liang Fa ordained first Protestant pastor of China
1825	American Tract Society formed
1829	Abolition of slavery in Mexico
1830	*Book of Mormon* published
1833	Slaves legally freed in Britain
1837	Mount Holyoke Female Seminary opens
1843	Fidelia Fiske sails to Persia
1844	First message in Morse Code sent over the wire by telegraph
1845	British Parliament passes *Lunacy Act*
1846	Mexican-American War begins
1850	Hong Xiuquan stirs up the Taiping Rebellion
1851	Sojourner Truth delivers famous "Ain't I a Woman?" speech
1852	*First Hindoo Convert: A Memoir of Krishna Pal published*; David Livingstone begins expedition for African east-west passage; *Uncle Tom's Cabin* published by Harriet Beecher Stowe
1859	Charles Darwin publishes *On the Origin of Species*
1865	Hudson Taylor founds China Inland Missions

What was the Awakening Church?

TO AWAKEN OR revive is to bring a dead person to life or rouse a sleeping person from slumber. You might think that after the Protestant Reformation in the sixteenth and seventeenth centuries, there could be no more spiritual death or slumber, right? Unfortunately, human beings—even Christian ones—are not very good at achieving balance. Reformers had called the church to stop abusing its power and correct its doctrinal errors. But after all those theological disputes and wars of religion, some ministers were concerned that Christians had started to identify themselves by which group they belonged to—instead of their individual relationships with God. They feared people had been distracted from whole-heartedly loving God because they were so busy fighting for God. When these ministers began to call sinners back from their spiritual death to cling to the life of the Spirit of God, *revivals* broke out on both sides of the Atlantic Ocean. These revivals lasted for decades and are now remembered as the *Great Awakenings*.

ENLIGHTENMENT AND DEISM

The Reformation movements had led to great changes, but also great bloodshed. By the eighteenth century, many people looked back on these wars as the result of religious oppression. They never wanted such tragic events to occur again. So in reaction, a new way of thinking began to develop, an era known as the Enlightenment. These thinkers believed all religion was superstitious, perhaps even a danger to society. As long as human beings imposed books like the Bible on others, they argued, there will always be wars and bloodshed. They said humans should live by the light of reason and nature instead of the Bible or other religious documents.

Some of these Enlightenment thinkers still believed in God. But they rejected the idea that God interfered supernaturally in the world or that by his Spirit he inspired human beings to write down his words. They called themselves *Deists*. They said that to believe in a Bible that can only be properly interpreted by the help of the Holy Spirit would give the person doing the interpreting an advantage over others. Instead, they believed when God created the world, he put in nature everything we needed to know about good and bad, life and liberty. So they set the Bible aside.

A lot of ministers preached against the ideas of the Deists. Some opposed extremes of any kind and called for toleration and middle ground. Others saw this as a compromise of Christian beliefs and called for a return to the Reformation view of justification by faith alone. They hoped for a revival of religion—and they got one. When the *First Great Awakening* occurred, it, like the Reformation, turned the world upside down.

THE FIRST GREAT AWAKENING

The decade of the 1730s was an important one for Protestant Christians in America and Great Britain.

In America, young Jonathan Edwards (1703-1758) grew up in a family of preachers. He had been taught that he would know exactly when he was converted, because all believers went through a process, including a part they called "humiliation" or fear of God's judgment. But try as he might, Jonathan never felt this way. Instead, when he repented of his sins, he simply trusted in Christ's righteousness to cover his sins. He discovered that in his trust he had less fear and more joy. The beauty of God and God's way of salvation by Christ had changed his heart.

By the early 1730s, Jonathan had become a minister at a church in Northampton, Massachusetts. He was concerned that many people were trusting in their own godly fear and righteousness for salvation, instead of looking to Christ. So in late 1734 he began preaching a series of sermons on justification by faith alone, telling his congregation about the kind of conversion he had experienced. People responded. A revival broke out that soon spread to surrounding towns. When ministers around the globe heard about it, they hoped for the same thing to happen in their churches.

Meanwhile, across the Atlantic, two brothers named John (1703-1791) and Charles (1707-1788) Wesley left England and sailed to Savannah, Georgia to minister to Native Americans. John was serving God, but like Jonathan Edwards, he never felt absolutely sure of his salvation. During his sea voyage to America, the weather turned nasty and everyone feared the ship would sink. But some Moravian ministers on board kept singing hymns, telling John they did not fear death because they were certain they would be with God for eternity. John wished he could believe the same about himself.

On May 24, 1738, after he had returned to England, he experienced a remarkable conversion. At a meeting on Aldersgate Street in London, he listened to a reading of Martin Luther's preface to the book of Romans and felt his heart "strangely warmed." He realized that he needed to trust in justification as the Reformers taught it. Through his preaching, he became the most important leader of the Methodist movement.

By 1740, revivals were happening on both sides of the Atlantic, led by Jonathan Edwards in America, John Wesley in England, and other powerful preachers like George Whitefield (1714-1770), who preached on both continents. These revivals became the First Great Awakening. And out of this widespread change of heart arose a new movement that would be called *Evangelicalism*.

THE EVANGELICALS

Evangelicals are those that preach the "good news" of salvation by Christ. The heirs of the Reformation, Evangelicals of the First Great Awakening called others to embrace the Reformation teaching of salvation by faith in Christ alone. They were members of different denominations who sometimes disagreed with each other on certain points of doctrine. For example, Jonathan Edwards was a Calvinist in the Congregational denomination, and John Wesley was an Arminian in the Anglican Church—meaning they held to different teachings on the ability of the human will to choose God—but they worked together to spread the gospel of Jesus Christ around the world.

Instead of ignoring the new ideas of the Enlightenment as some Christians did, Evangelicals interacted with them, offering a vital Christianity as an alternative to Deism or atheism. Contrary to the Deists, they called everyone to embrace the Bible as the divine and authoritative Word of God.

Their teachings emphasized conversion, and that salvation comes only through Christ and not human works. They believed God's Spirit could revive the world from the deadness of sin and awaken the church out of its slumber. They believed it was their duty to actively tell others about their beliefs, through evangelism, missions, and charitable works. For these reasons, they continued to seek new revivals. When the fires of the First Great Awakening eventually died down, Evangelicals hoped for another one.

THE SECOND GREAT AWAKENING

The ideas of Jonathan Edwards and John Wesley carried on into the next generation of Evangelicals. In the 1790s, Timothy Dwight (1752-1817), the president of Yale College and a minister in the tradition of Jonathan Edwards, led a revival in local churches that spread into New York. It was carried on there by the work of a lawyer-turned-preacher named Charles Grandison Finney (1792-1875) after his conversion in 1821. That revival led to others, and at the same time, revivals were also breaking out in the Southern United States. These events became known as the *Second Great Awakening*.

As before, the Evangelicals active in these revivals came from diverse backgrounds and locations. But they united around their great emphasis on conversion. Many Evangelicals, especially Methodist followers of John Wesley in England, called for social changes that reflected a renewed Christian life. For example, they were active in ending slavery, improving the conditions of hospitals and prisons, and educating the poor. You will read a lot more about these efforts later in this book.

By the 1850s, the intensity of the Second Great Awakening had faded, but the work of Evangelicals continued on. Today, a large percentage of Christians from many different denominations identify themselves as Evangelicals because they emphasize the same things as their Awakenings ancestors: conversion, the power of the Holy Spirit to change hearts, a duty to spread the gospel, and involvement in social reform.

FINDING THE TRUE STORY

The stories in this book, covering the years of 1700 to 1860, chronicle what could be the most unique, diverse, and influential movement in the history of the church. Why did we choose these particular characters instead of the many other Evangelicals of that period? It is not because the characters in these stories always had correct doctrine or made fewer mistakes than others in their service to God! Like all human beings, sometimes they got it right and sometimes they messed up. That is why it is not wise to think of them as heroes. But God used them anyway, and their efforts became some of the most important in the Evangelical story. They are statesmen (William Wilberforce), philanthropists (Elizabeth Fry), explorers (David Livingstone), former slaves (Sojourner Truth), writers (Harriet Beecher Stowe), pastors (Jonathan Edwards, John Wesley, Liang Fa), and missionaries (William Carey, Adoniram and Ann Judson, Fidelia Fiske). They are women and men, educated and illiterate, from every ethnicity, class, and age. They were active in the world, willing to engage every trial for the spread of their "good news."

We have also included the story of Johann Sebastian Bach, who would not have called himself an Evangelical. He was a Lutheran Christian active in the days at the very beginning of the Awakenings, before Evangelicalism came to be. But the work that he did to develop music within a vital Christianity helped make music a more significant part of worship in the church. This would be very important to later Evangelical movements, who used music as a method of preaching the gospel. And his story helps to show that during the Great Awakenings, people who did not agree with all the Evangelical ideals were still active for the gospel. Christians who, for example, thought the revivals were too enthusiastic, still called for renewed dedication to Christ. Christians from every tradition continued to proclaim the gospel during these years in the ways they believed were appropriate.

These are stories of real Christians, taken from their diaries, letters, and books. From them we learn that during the First and Second Great Awakenings, Christians became more and more concerned about living Christianly, not just believing Christianly. God used the tender hearts—and the strong hands—of his people to offer mercy to the world.

JONATHAN EDWARDS:
AN INWARD SWEET SENSE

WINTER 1734. NORTHAMPTON, MASSACHUSETTS.

A BITING WIND blasted the rickety fence, bending the pickets into submission. Snow crystals traced swirling paths around the corner of the meeting house and on through the crack in the door.

"Brrrr!" shuddered a woman inside as she passed in front of the entrance. She wiped the melting flakes from her dark hair and the front of her blue wool dress. "Jonathan, we need to have that door repaired. It's cold enough in here without inviting the snow."

The tall man looked up at her with a distracted expression. He was adjusting his black clerical robes and the white wig that ministers and politicians wore as a sign of authority. As he straightened it, the wind caught the powdered curls and bounced them against his cheeks, leaving faint white scuffs on his jaw.

The woman chuckled and brushed the powder from his face. "Apparently the wind is as fond of that ugly thing as I am."

Jonathan flashed a brief smile at her. "Sarah, not the wig complaints again! But you are right about this door. I will raise the question about fixing it to the congregation. I would not want the cold wind to interfere with the message of the gospel."

Sarah put out her hands to warm them above a bank of candles. "The people of Northampton are trusting in Christ like never before. I dare say that a biting wind will not keep them from being here tonight, my dear."

"God is indeed blessing the message of salvation by Christ alone." He drew near her to warm his hands too, and then after a moment added, "I fear, though, that one day the people of New England will trust in themselves rather than God."

She had to fully extend her arm to put a hand on her husband's shoulder. Her voice was low. "Preach what you know to be true, Jonathan, and trust the Spirit of God to do the work."

He gazed into her eyes. The warm light she saw there told her he was grateful for her encouragement.

He moved away to find a place to pray. It was his custom to spend time in quiet prayer before every sermon. The service would begin in about an hour, and congregation members would start to arrive soon. Many of them came early to confess their sins to God in silence before the public service began.

Kneeling in his family's pew, he made a mental list of people in his church who had recently professed faith in Jesus. As their faces came into his mind, he thought of their conversion stories, each as different as the people themselves. When he was younger he thought every person's conversion was supposed to look the same, and it had tortured him for many years. But now he saw it differently. As Jonathan thought about the new converts in his church, he was flooded with memories of his childhood.

Like most kids, Jonathan and his friends liked to play make believe. But they didn't pretend they were cowboys rounding up cattle or explorers crossing a new river. These boys pretended to be theologians. They built prayer booths where they prayed five times a day and got into long debates about the Bible. Jonathan's father, Timothy Edwards, and his grandfather, Solomon Stoddard, were preachers, and little Jonathan wanted to be spiritual like them. But it was a lot harder than it looked.

His mother and father were always reminding him that unless he trusted in Christ, he would face eternal punishment for his sins. "Remember what we told you about how many people died during King Philip's War?" his mother said more than once. "You never know when another Indian raid will happen against our town. God doesn't promise anyone another day on earth. A wise boy will be ready to meet God at any moment."

"Why would God send a person like me to hell?" he once asked his father. "I have no desire to be his enemy."

"You are a sinner, Jonathan, like all people. The sinner has offended a perfect and infinite God. He must pay a price that equals the crime. His only escape is conversion."

"But how can I know I have been converted?"

His father leaned in and gave him a piercing look. "You will fear our righteous God. You will feel convicted of your sins, and you will turn away from them."

Jonathan wanted to be a Christian, but he just didn't feel like one most of the time. "If I pray long enough and hard enough," he thought, "maybe then I will be a true Christian." But his religious feelings wore off so easily. Every time he thought, "yes, I am truly a Christian now," he found himself talking back to his mother or having an urge to punch one of his ten sisters. A Christian wouldn't do that, would he?

"I was so confused back then," Jonathan remembered as he knelt on the hard floor of the church, preparing for the service. "For all my efforts, I was trusting in myself to live up to God's expectations. I didn't understand how serious my sin was and what it meant to trust in Christ's righteousness."

He glanced up as he heard the shuffling of congregation members arriving at the back. "I only hope that my sermon tonight will allow my congregation to know Christ as I have come to know him." He opened the large Bible in his hands and flipped through the worn, finger-stained pages.

"Ah, here it is," he thought, setting the open book down on the pew in front of him. "1 Timothy 1:17." The passage was a special one for him. As he closed his eyes, his memory opened up again.

He was a student at Yale College. The school had received a fine collection of books for their library, and Jonathan had never seen so many in one place—over 800 volumes filled the wooden crates! Some were very old, with broken spines and scribbled notes in the margins. Others were freshly printed, donated by the authors themselves. He was anxious to read them all.

Standing among the crates, he took out one of the volumes. A paper slipped to the floor. When he bent to pick it up, he noticed a signature.

"Isaac Newton?" he mumbled in surprise. "The famous scientist donated books to our school?" He began to scan the pages, looking at mathematical equations and geometrical figures. Soon he was so engrossed that he didn't hear the footsteps behind him.

"What are you reading, Jonathan?"

He spun around. "Oh, hello, Mr. Cutler. I...I was just—."

"Reading the greats, I see," the school rector replied in his booming voice. In contrast to Jonathan's thin frame and sharp features, Mr. Cutler was round with a fleshy nose and double chin.

"Yes, sir. I have not read Newton before."

"Many fine theologians have yet to read Newton."

Jonathan held out the volume to Mr. Cutler, but the rector raised a hand in protest. "No, no, take the book and continue reading. I'd like you to report back to me on it later."

"Yes, sir."

"You are a bright student, Jonathan," Mr. Cutler continued. "You have a lot of promise. I think you will one day do great things for the church."

"Thank you, sir," Jonathan said. "Lord willing," he added. But he still wondered if he was really a Christian doing the Lord's will.

Mr. Cutler turned to go, but paused and said, "You may as well know that I wrote your father and told him my high opinion of you. Keep up the fine work. I look forward to your report."

Jonathan had always loved to read, but now he was really excited about the additions to Yale's library. He began reading the new books on the Bible and kept asking himself "Who is God?" and "What is God really like?" and "How can a human being understand a divine being?"

When summer came, he took some of the books home with him to his parents' house in East Windsor, Connecticut. One warm afternoon, while he was studying Newton in his room, he picked up his Bible. Opening it to 1 Timothy 1:17, he read: "Now unto the King eternal, immortal, invisible, the only wise God, be honor and glory forever and ever. Amen."

Jonathan had heard these words spoken in church and read them himself so many times. But today, they sounded different.

"Immortal," he pondered. "Invisible. Eternal king and wise God. Worthy of unending honor and glory." The words kept echoing in his mind. He was suddenly seized with a sweet sense of God's presence in his soul. Smiling, he jumped up and hurried out of the house. He always worked out his thoughts by taking a walk.

"Such beautiful words!" he thought, repeating the verse again and again. That he could know God, the eternally wise one who deserves all glory, seemed remarkable to Jonathan. "How excellent a being God must be, and how happy I will be if he takes me up to be with him in his heaven when I die!"

He scanned the blue skies as he bounded through the fields, noticing every butterfly, every birdsong, every seedpod carried by the breeze. Each one seemed to shout God's presence. "I've never felt this way before," he marveled. "It is as if the world around me is declaring God's beauty."

Coming upon a stone wall marking the edge of a field, he kneeled there in the grass. "Great God," he prayed aloud, "if I can enjoy you so much just walking through your creation and pondering your being, let me enjoy you for eternity. I trust you. I want to be swallowed up in your presence. I want to be captivated by your beauty and love."

With greater vigor than before, he threw himself into his studies. He scoured his father's library for commentaries that explained the Bible. He read every book about grace, about salvation, about the excellency of Christ. He read Newton to learn more about the universe that revealed God's beauty. He learned that every atom of the world is sustained by God's mighty hand. Every day he was fascinated by what he discovered.

After dinner one night, Jonathan sat at the table with his father.

"Mr. Cutler tells me he is pleased with your studies," Timothy said. "You are a disciplined scholar."

"He is a good leader," Jonathan replied modestly. "He commands the respect of the students."

"He says he has taken you under his care."

"Yes. He gives me books to read and watches over my progress."

Timothy nodded. "You've spent much time walking in the fields lately. Are you concerned about something?"

"I have been pondering God's majesty and beauty."

"Ah, is that all!" Timothy looked at his son with respectful amusement.

Jonathan paused. "Father, I believe I now love Christ the way I always hoped to as a child."

Timothy was instantly serious. He leaned forward in his chair. "You have felt convicted of sin and your need for Christ?"

Jonathan answered slowly and deliberately. "I have felt convicted, yes, but more so I have felt love for Christ. I am enjoying the presence of God on my long walks."

He was used to his father raising his eyebrows. But this time it seemed he was trying to open his eyes wide enough to peer into his son's soul.

"Have you experienced the fear of God?" Timothy demanded

"Not so much fear as great joy in Christ."

"But also humility before God and the gravity of your eternal condition?"

"I feel humble before God because of his greatness. I feel joy at the thought of being with him for eternity. I know I deserve hell, but Jesus has paid for it, and the shame pales compared to my joy."

Timothy sat back in his chair with a "hmmm," and then was quiet.

"My experience is not a terror of eternal punishment, the way you and Grandfather Stoddard have described it," Jonathan said. "Instead, I have an inward sweet sense that God's glory is in everything. That his wisdom, as is spoken of in the book of 1 Timothy, is reflected in the physical world—in the sun, moon, stars, clouds, grass, flowers...."

His father was frowning at him.

"Father," he went on, "remember how I used to be afraid of thunderstorms? But now I know, really know, that God is in control of all things. My mind is somehow different."

Timothy looked him straight in the eye. "This is not the normal way of true conversion, my son."

Jonathan was confused and disappointed. He had expected his father to rejoice at his news. "Then you believe I have yet to find God?"

"All I am saying is that when you were a child you thought you knew Christ. Don't let yourself be fooled again, Jonathan. To see God in this world is one thing; to live for him with fervent holiness is another. Be careful not to confuse the two. The destiny of your soul is at stake."

That night, Jonathan slipped out to the meadow and lay down in the grass. He stared up at the pinpoints of starlight in the dark sky. He listened to the insects calling out to each other in the trees. And he prayed that God would assure him of his salvation.

Jonathan never could have guessed how God would answer his prayer over the next year.

It started with a scandal at Yale. When Jonathan returned to college in September, Rector Cutler shocked everyone at the commencement service by quoting from the Book of Common Prayer, used by the Anglican church. Yale was not an Anglican school. Rumors quickly spread that Mr. Cutler had rejected the Reformed doctrine taught at Yale, that he had become Anglican or even Catholic. The trustees dismissed him. Jonathan was confused by his teacher's change of doctrine and sorry to see him go.

Winter arrived. Jonathan began to prepare for his graduation the following fall. He decided to get some practical experience by preaching for a few months at a church in New York that was looking for a new pastor. A light snow was collecting outside his parents' house as he packed his bags for New York.

"I'm pleased with your choice," said his father from the door of his room. "This church experience will be good for you while you write your Master's thesis for graduation."

Jonathan looked up from the pile of books and clothes on his bed. "I think so, too," he said. "And it will be good to get away from the mess Mr. Cutler created."

"I assume you have heard that Yale students and professors are now required to sign the Saybrook Confession of Faith," said Timothy. "They are going to examine all students carefully to make sure they have sound doctrine before they graduate."

"Then I better do well on my thesis," Jonathan nodded.

"You were one of Cutler's favorite students. They certainly will be looking for any sign that you were corrupted by his teachings."

"Yes, sir."

"And they are right to do so, my son. Any man who seeks to be a pastor must understand the nature of true salvation. Be sure you do." And he walked away.

"How can I know what to say in my exam if my own father questions my salvation? And Mr. Cutler's too?" he asked himself quietly. He knew his experience was different from his father's, and yet he believed it was sincere.

He reached for a small notebook. Over the last few months he had started writing notes to himself. He called them his "resolutions." As a child, whenever he thought he was truly a Christian, he fell back into his sins. He knew now that no one was perfect. But he also believed that a life of godly behavior might be a sign that his heart was truly saved. So he began to write down his resolutions for Christian behavior.

Opening the book, he read: "Resolved, never to do anything out of revenge." He hoped that by reading this often he might keep himself from regretful action.

This time he penned another. "Resolved," he wrote. He paused for a minute to consider how he should phrase his words, then inked his pen and continued. "Constantly and diligently and with the strictest scrutiny, to look into the state of my soul, that I may know whether I have truly an interest in Christ or not."

The next several months, he devoted all of his studies to this goal. During his time in New York, Jonathan discovered that he loved to preach. He was not twenty years old, yet he was responsible for the spiritual needs of a congregation. It was even more important now that he know what true salvation looked like. He spent every day in his study, reading the Bible and books about the Bible. At night he went for quiet walks on the banks of the Hudson River.

In April, the church hired a permanent pastor and Jonathan went back to his home in East Windsor. All spring and summer he wrote in his notebooks and prepared for his final exam at Yale. His father wanted to know what topic he would write his thesis on.

"Luther, Calvin, and all those who embraced the reformation of the church taught that my salvation before God was not my own doing," Jonathan explained. "Jesus is the only one who can save me. So I am going to write my thesis on the doctrine of justification by faith alone because of Christ alone."

"Well, my son does not shy from challenges!" declared Timothy.

"The Yale board will want to know that I still hold to the doctrines of grace," reminded Jonathan. "I plan to show them I know those doctrines very well."

"I hope that you believe them in your heart as much as you know them in your head!" was his father's reply.

Summer wore on, and Jonathan spent it writing his thesis and preaching at various churches. He was worried that he would say something wrong about justification and they wouldn't let him graduate. Sometimes he went to New Haven so he could use the Yale library. Rainy days spent hunched over his books left him depressed. But when the sun came out, he stretched his long legs walking around New Haven. There were plenty of places to walk in town and in the woods. Being outside where he could pray and walk lifted his spirits.

One Saturday afternoon, Jonathan left his books on the library table and stepped outside to take in some fresh air. He made his way through town at a brisk pace, feeling the muscles in his calves warm with the exercise. In his mind, he could see the sentences of his thesis that he had written that morning. As he walked, the words would rearrange themselves. He occasionally stopped and made a note on the slips of paper he kept clipped inside his coat.

It was too nice outside to go back in the library. When the brick street ended, he kept going, eventually turning off the dirt road into a pasture. He hadn't gone far when he saw someone coming down the path at the edge of the woods. It was a young woman in a yellow dress.

He recognized the face when she got closer. It was Sarah Pierpont, whose father was the pastor of the Congregationalist church in New Haven. Jonathan sometimes worshiped there when he was in town. His father had talked about the Pierpont family, and mentioned Sarah by name. He had described her as a Christian who could not be persuaded to do anything wrong because her love for God was so strong.

She didn't appear to have noticed Jonathan yet. She was close enough that he could hear snatches of singing and then gentle conversation. But she had no companion. Who was she talking to?

"Good afternoon, Miss Pierpont," Jonathan said, pausing on the path and removing his hat.

She stopped in mid-song, but wasn't startled. "Hello, Mr. Edwards. Isn't it a glorious day for a walk?"

"It is," he agreed. "What was that you were singing?"

Sarah laughed and drew nearer. Now he could see that her dark hair was pulled back with a brown silk ribbon. Her eyes were shining and her cheeks were flushed like she had been deep in conversation. "Oh, I sometimes make up little songs as I walk. If the birds can praise God in the woods, so can I."

"You come out to the woods to pray?"

She smiled. "The beauty of nature reminds me of the beauty of God," she explained. "I meditate on that out here and he fills me with such a sweet delight that I hardly care for anything else."

He stared at her, not rudely, but with admiration. "Do you ever feel that he might just carry you up to heaven right out of these woods?"

Now she was startled. "Well, yes, sometimes I do feel that way. I know he loves me too much to keep me at a distance forever." Then she blushed. "I've never admitted that to anyone before."

"But I know just what you mean," he offered quickly. "It is a great joy to love and be loved by the invisible almighty God who rules the world."

"Indeed!"

They gazed at one another until they both felt awkward.

"Well," said Jonathan. He put his hat back on and gave her a formal nod. "It is rude of me to keep you from your walk."

"It was good to see you, Mr. Edwards. I wish you success with your exams at Yale."

"Thank you."

She moved on down the path. Jonathan watched her for a moment and soon heard her singing again. When she disappeared, he leaned against a tree and pulled paper and a stick of graphite from his coat.

"There is a young lady in New Haven," he jotted down. "She is of a wonderful sweetness, calmness, and benevolence of mind, especially after those seasons in which this great God has manifested himself to her mind. She seems to be full of joy and pleasure, and no one knows for what."

"But I understand," he said to himself, sliding the paper back inside his coat.

And then the thought came to him so suddenly and powerfully that he leaned against the tree again. After all these years, he had found the answer to his searching. He finally knew, once and for all, that he was saved!

He knew, because Scripture told him Jesus had paid for his sins, and he believed it. He knew, because God had given him great joy and wonder in his presence. And he had just heard Sarah talk about her sweet communion with God. She wasn't terrified of God. Just the opposite! She deeply loved him, like Jonathan did, and yet she was sure of her salvation.

"I struggled because I started with a false assumption," he realized aloud, shaking his head. "I assumed, and so did my father, that my conversion was supposed to be just like his. But God speaks to different hearts in different ways! My father turned to God because he saw the darkness of his own heart compared to

God's holiness and he feared for his soul. I turned to God because I was raptured by his beauty and power and knew I could love and trust him. We're both right! God is so vast and amazing that he can draw us to him with different aspects of his being."

Jonathan nearly began to sing too, overwhelmed with a God who deserved both fear and love. He bounded back down the path, eager to return to the library.

Renewed, he soon finished writing his thesis. When the time came for his examination, the Yale board declared him an excellent scholar and a fine Christian ready to serve the church. After graduation, Jonathan became a minister. And four years later, he married Sarah Pierpont.

Now Sarah was re-lighting candles at the back of the church where his Grandfather Stoddard used to be the minister. The flames kept going out as the wind followed the congregation inside. The pews were nearly full. Most of the people were on their knees or leaning forward in their seats, quietly preparing to hear Reverend Edwards's sermon.

Jonathan rose to his feet and carried his Bible to the back, where Sarah was waiting for him to escort her to their pew.

"Are you ready to preach?" she asked softly.

He nodded and took her arm. But instead of stepping forward, he drew her aside. "Do you remember the little piece I wrote about you before we were married?"

She smiled. "Of course. It was beautiful."

"It was your example that the Lord used to show me the nature of true conversion. That is what I will preach on tonight."

"Since then he has used you to teach me so much about who he is," she whispered back. "And now your congregation waits for you to expound his beauty to them, too. Tell them why they must give their hearts to God."

He gave her that intense look again, took his Bible firmly in both hands, and went up to the pulpit.

That winter, Jonathan Edwards preached a series of sermons on justification by faith alone, which started a great revival in New England. The revival even spread to Europe, and made him internationally famous.

Two of his most famous writings are "Sinners in the Hands of an Angry God" and "A Treatise Concerning Religious Affections," showing his belief in God's terrifying holiness as well as God's sweet love. It was his struggle for conversion and desire to understand God better that gave him such a powerful message and drew others to hear him preach.

Jonathan is considered by many to be the greatest American theologian. When he died on March 22, 1758, of complications from a smallpox inoculation, he was president of the College of New Jersey, which would later be renamed Princeton University. Sarah died October 2 of the same year.

JOHANN SEBASTIAN BACH: SOLI DEO GLORIA

APRIL 1736. LEIPZIG, GERMANY.

PEOPLE SAID THE household of Johann Sebastian Bach was like a pigeon coop. Sun-up to sundown, it was full of activity. The cantor of St. Thomas Church had a large family with a new baby almost every year. It was colorful, too. Local musicians streamed in and out of the house, their powdered wigs and long coat-tails fluttering like plumage. And it was noisy. Strains of music bubbled down onto the street from the upper windows all day long.

Each day in Cantor Bach's coop began early with the screech of a rooster on the roof. Bach dressed quickly in the murky light: blouse, hose, breeches, vest, jacket, shoes, pocketwatch. He went down to the first floor to use the privy at the back of the building. Then he slipped back upstairs to his composing studio and knelt under the window to say his morning prayers.

By the time he rose and looked out the window, the sun was high enough to illuminate the countryside to the west. From his rooms, built into the city wall, he had a good view of the Pleisse

River coursing toward the castle of Merseburg in the distance. It looked quiet outside the city, but inside the cantor's five-story apartment the day's activities were getting underway.

On the first floor, the younger Bach children gathered with their tutor in the largest room for their grammar lessons. One of them would be charged with answering the door all morning as students arrived at regular intervals, climbing the stairs to the cantor's studio for their private music lessons. The maid was busy scrubbing tablecloths in the washroom at the back of the house. She would soon be carrying her damp burden past all five floors up to the drying room in the highest attic.

On the second floor, the cantor's oldest daughter, Catharina, moved between the kitchen and the dining room, laying out two dozen silver spoons and a coffee set on the sideboard. She chatted with the cook as she worked. As usual, the family would be joined at lunch by a number of guests.

Across the hall in the music library, Bach's wife and older sons had gathered around the work tables to copy out manuscripts of the cantor's latest composition. Each member of the church choir and orchestra would need a copy for rehearsal on Saturday and then the service on Sunday. Mrs. Anna Magdalena Bach hummed as she inked in the notes on large sheets of manuscript paper. She had been a professional singer when she met her husband, and people still requested her services at their weddings and funerals. But she spent most of her time managing the household and providing musical assistance to her husband.

And in his studio, Cantor Bach knew today would be as busy as usual. He drank a mug of coffee at his desk while he made a few notes to his schedule. From 7:00 to 10:00 he would give private lessons in his studio and lecture students at the St. Thomas School next door. At 11:00, he would join his household for a one-hour lunch, then go back to the classroom for daily singing exercises until 1:00. Afternoons were for composing, repairing and tuning instruments at home and the church, letter writing, and other business. Dinner, with more guests, would be served promptly at 6:00.

If that wasn't enough responsibility, every four weeks, the cantor was in charge of evening rounds at the St. Thomas School, leading evening prayers and meeting with students. Fortunately, this was not one of those weeks, so he could spend the hours after dinner tonight making music with his family and guests.

Rising from his desk, he crossed the studio to the harpsichord. He had noticed the night before that it was out of tune. So he opened the wooden case and bent over the long row of taut strings. In fifteen minutes, he had made the necessary adjustments and was ready for the first knock at his door.

"*Guten tag*, Gottfried," he said when the boy entered.

"Hello, Herr Bach." Gottfried went right to his place at the keyboard.

"Begin," said the cantor from his desk chair.

For twenty minutes, Gottfried played through his assignments, pausing when the cantor called out a correction.

"Your left hand fingering is clumsy," Bach said, rising. "You must think smarter to improve it. Here, I have written a piece just for you to train the deficient fingers." He propped a sheet of manuscript paper on the ledge above the keys and pointed. "Begin."

With his brow wrinkled in concentration, Gottfried worked his way through the new exercise. He shook his head when he finished. "This piece highlights all my weaknesses."

"That is just the idea," said Bach. "Identify the weak fingers, strengthen them by repetition, and then everything you play will be much improved." He tapped his finger on the paper. "Again."

Gottfried took a deep breath and began the piece again. Herr Bach made him play it five times before he slid the page from the stand and handed it to the boy.

"Now the viola," directed the cantor.

Gottfried rose from the bench. Opening the slim case he had

carried in with him, he lifted out the wooden instrument. He tightened the bow, ran it across the pot of rosin to smooth the bow hairs, and then touched it to the strings.

The viola sang, a rapid melody of a hymn often sung in the Lutheran service. Cantor Bach listened with his eyes closed, his jowls vibrating as he followed the music with his chin. He said nothing until Gottfried had finished.

"The viola is your instrument," he said with feeling when he opened his eyes again. "You must practice more slowly, learn to be more precise before you jump into performance tempo. But you have a gift." After a pause, his voice was stern. "However, proficiency on the harpsichord is absolutely necessary!"

"Yes, Herr Bach."

"Good. That is all."

Gottfried carefully tucked the sheet of music into his viola case with the instrument. But at the door, he paused and looked back.

"Herr Bach?"

His teacher looked up from his desk. "Yes?"

"Herr Bach, why did you decide to become a musician?"

"I didn't decide, my boy, God did. I was born into a family of musicians in Eisenach."

"Eisenach? Where the great Dr. Luther went to school?"

"Why, yes. In fact, I attended the same Latin school as Luther, though of course many years later. In Eisenach, my father was a violinist and town musician, just like his father before him and many of my uncles. For years the dukes have had Bachs as their court musicians. So my way was clear from my earliest days."

He began to turn away, but then a thought occurred to him. "That is not to say that I have just carried on with destiny, my boy. You see, God made me a musician, but I chose to develop my gifts. What could be more glorious than music? It thrills the soul. And a church musician has a powerful role."

"Speaking of Dr. Luther," he said, opening a drawer in his desk and pulling out a large German Bible. "Here is his translation of the Holy Scripture. Look at this."

It took him only a moment to find the passage he was looking for. "The second book of Chronicles, chapter five: 'The trumpeters and singers joined in unison, as with one voice, to give praise and thanks to the Lord. Accompanied by trumpets, cymbals and other instruments, they raised their voices in praise to the Lord and sang, He is good; his love endures forever. Then the temple of the Lord was filled with a cloud, and the priests could not perform their service because of the cloud, for the glory of the Lord filled the temple of God.'"

"Do you know what I learn from this?" said Cantor Bach. "I learn that where there is devotional music, God is always at hand with his gracious presence."

He shut the heavy Bible with a thump and returned it to the drawer. "A careless performance squanders God's beautiful gift and displeases him. That is why we pursue musical excellence. Speaking of which, you have much work to do. I expect you to have perfected the fingering I showed you by next week!"

"Yes, Herr Bach," the teenager said, scrambling to the door. "Good day."

Gottfried's lesson was followed by another. When his last student of the morning left, the cantor crossed the hallway and let himself into the library. Anna was still at work copying, her full sleeves rolled up to keep them from dragging through the ink.

"*Guten tag*, my dear." He stooped to kiss the top of her head and glanced down at the manuscript. "How grateful I am for your clear handwriting."

"I will have all the copies you need of this one by tomorrow afternoon," she said. "How were your lessons?"

"Fine," he said distractedly. He had pulled a wide sheaf of manuscript paper from one of the slots lining the library wall. The book was titled "The Little Organ Book," and on the cover page he had long ago scrawled a poem: "In praise of the Almighty's will and for my neighbor's greater skill." It was a collection of pieces for building a student's proficiency, like the one he had written for Gottfried. But these were to be played on a pipe organ. He was thinking of sending a copy of the book to a friend who was an organist in another city.

Anna was still looking at him. "Don't you have a lecture now?" she reminded.

"Oh, yes. I am on my way, dear." He decided to pick up the book on his way back to the studio later, and slid it back into the slot. "See you at luncheon."

On the opposite side of the library, he unlocked a door that led from his apartment into a classroom on the second floor of the St. Thomas School. Two of the boys were already seated, and the rest of the class joined them a few minutes later via the school entrance.

This week he was lecturing on organ building.

"The pipe organ is the most complex machine in the world," he declared. "It takes two people to work this machine, the bellows operator and the organist. When the bellows operator pumps the bellows, air is forced into the long flat wind chest. On top of the wind chest sits rows of pipes in every size, from the length of my finger to the length of this wall, one pipe for every key on the keyboard."

Normally, he rested his hands in his upper vest pockets when he lectured, unless he needed to gesture. This lecture required lots of gesturing.

"When the organist pulls a 'stop' on the console, a particular set of pipes is given access to the air. Each key is connected to a valve on the pipe, so that when the organist presses the key, the valve opens, air whistles through the pipe, and the sound is born."

His arms were everywhere now, and his eyes glowed. He always became animated when he was talking about his favorite instrument.

"What makes the organ special," he went on, "is that each one is unique. No two organs are ever the same, because they are built specifically for the space they inhabit. Only the best engineers become organ builders. They have to think about the size and shape of the room, where the console will be placed, the number and types of sound the organist wants to make, and how much money the church is willing to spend for materials and time. So you see, it is a very complex and expensive instrument. And there is nothing more glorious than the music it produces!"

Cantor Bach did not need notes to give this lecture. Besides his reputation as a skilled organist, he was also known throughout Germany as the best organ examiner. Before a newly-built organ was performed, the church hired Bach to test all the stops, to crawl between the pipes and inspect the craftsmanship, to make sure the bellows took in enough air. He gave them a written report with recommendations to the organ builder, and often played the first public concert on the new instrument.

So a lecture by Cantor Bach on the subject of organ building was a great privilege for the students. That is why they were especially excited when he announced they would spend the rest of the hour inside the organ at St. Thomas Church. If they took great care, he promised, he might even pull out one of the pipes and let them examine it.

When he appeared in the dining room at 11:00, his face was shining with pleasure. He was also covered in dust, and Anna made him wash up in the kitchen before he sat at her table. The older children were already seated, along with the apprentice who was currently boarding with them, and a theology professor who taught at St. Thomas. The Bach table always had room for visitors.

An hour later, he was back at the school leading a singing class all the students were required to attend. On special occasions they added their voices to the professional musicians in the church choir, so vocal exercises were part of their daily training.

And then his final class of the day was over. He took a glass of brandy into his studio and sat down at his writing desk. Today he needed to compose a new chorale—a hymn text arranged for four parts—for the Sunday service. He got up from his desk only once, to look up something in a theological commentary by Luther. He did not go to the harpsichord until he was finished marking out all the notes on the page in front of him. Eyes closed, he played through the piece slowly, letting the final notes linger. Then with a flourish, he signed the bottom of the page: "Joh. Seb. Bach. *Soli Deo Gloria*." To God alone be glory.

The rest of the afternoon he spent catching up on business. When Anna knocked at the door, he had written and sealed two letters. One was about a future organ examination and the other to collect payment owed him for an instrument rental.

She had a list of household supplies in her hand, and pushed it across his desk as she sank into the other chair. "Here are the items to add to your order," she said. "We need more lye for the washing, and I think it will take 10 skeins of wool for the boys' new trousers. Plus, Catharina tells me you have taken to adding sugar to your coffee, so the kitchen is running low."

"You would begrudge an old man his sugar?"

She ignored the mischievous twinkle in his eye. "You are not old, Sebastian."

But he was not done teasing. "I have a twenty-five-year-old son."

"And a six-month-old son," she retorted.

His face became sober. "And how is little Johann Christian?"

"He seems to be strong," was all she said.

But her comment was enough to encourage him. A strong baby was more likely to survive the many childhood illnesses. They had already buried seven children in the last ten years.

"Speaking of sons," he hurried on, handing her an open letter from the pile of mail on his desk. "I have heard from the second oldest. It sounds like Carl is doing well at the University of Frankfurt."

"Wonderful!" She slipped the page into her pocket. "I will read it while I check on dinner preparations."

She left, and he went back to his work. By dinnertime, he was ready to exchange his solitude for a hearty meal and a concert in the parlor.

Tonight, the menu was cured ham, cabbage, and roasted potatoes. A lute player named Leopold was visiting from Dresden, and Cantor Bach had insisted he come to dinner. Leopold was soon joking and singing and passing dishes around the table like one of the family.

"I have to ask you," said Leopold when there was a break in the conversation. "In Dresden they still tell stories about how, years ago, you won a contest against the haughty Frenchman Louis Marchand. Is it true?"

Bach rolled his eyes. "Why does everyone ask me about that?"

"He hates to tell this story," said Anna, grinning. "But it is one of my favorites. So I always offer to tell it for him. Shall I, dear?"

"No, no," the cantor said firmly. "You embellish it when you tell it."

She pretended innocence. "Then I guess you'll have to recount it yourself!"

Bach looked from Anna to Leopold and saw they were not going to give up. "Fine!" he grunted. "The contest wasn't my idea. Louis Marchand, the celebrated clavier player, showed up in Dresden to play for the king. He was so good, the king immediately granted him a post as a royal musician. But Marchand was not the humblest of men. The concertmaster in Dresden at the time, a man named Volumier, was determined to prove to this Frenchman that Germany had produced her fair share of musical talent as well."

"Ah, that is how you came to be in Dresden," Leopold deduced.

Bach nodded. "Volumier prevailed upon me to challenge Marchand to a musical duel to perform any musical task, on the spot. As Volumier suspected, Marchand could not resist. So the place and time were set. When I arrived at the home of Count Flemming, where the contest was to take place, a great number of royals and other high-ranking people were present. They expected to get a great show out of it, of course. But after a long delay without the appearance of Marchand, the count sent someone to his apartment and…" He trailed off.

"And?"

"He had packed up and hired a carriage out of Dresden that morning!"

"Amazing! So the contest never took place?"

The cantor shook his head. "The crowd was so disappointed, having been promised a night of musical merriment. So I went ahead and played my best for several hours."

"And the king was very impressed with him," Anna jumped in.

Bach shrugged. "That is why people say I won the contest—it was only by default. Still, it was a shame for me to travel so far and for the court to waste all that wig powder and rouge for nothing."

"Ha!" bellowed Leopold. "Marchand must have been terrified that Germany would discover the inferiority of his French training!"

"Oh, but I had heard him play," Bach persisted. "He was really quite a fine musician."

Anna clucked at her husband. "Don't be so modest, Sebastian. Everyone knows you would have won the contest by far."

He waved his arms irritably. "I told you the story. Now I insist we change the subject."

Leopold grinned. "Well then, tell me—are the church politics as bad in Leipzig as they are in Dresden?"

"Now that is a topic I'd be glad to discuss!" Bach cried, leaning over his plate. "If it is not a dispute about theology around here, it is a dispute about money. For example, I firmly believe that God expects us to take as much care with our music as we do with our preaching. I have been trying to convince the city council to budget more money for musicians. I don't have enough professionals to play and sing all the necessary parts for a Sunday service. The council tells me to get student volunteers to do it——."

"Let me guess," Leopold interrupted. "But then they complain that the volunteers aren't as good."

"Exactly! Well, of course, I tell them, a man who is worried about how he will buy bread cannot focus on mastering his instrument!"

Leopold shook his head. "It makes no sense, I agree. However, such policies do not seem to have damaged the musical reputation of St. Thomas. I hear the Good Friday performance of your St. Matthew Passion was just astounding. 'A sermon in sound' is what they said."

"You are too kind, my friend. Music is, after all, another method of Scripture proclamation. But come now, tell me the news from Dresden."

So they shared political and musical news all the way through the apple cake for dessert.

"And now we must have a concert!" Bach declared as soon as the table was cleared. "If you have never heard Anna and Catharina sing, I promise you it will be a pleasure."

He didn't have to convince Anna to take her place at the center of the parlor. They were all natural performers and loved nothing more than making music together. Two of the boys sat down before the clavier in the corner. Anna and Catharina warmed up their voices. The apprentice hurried to his room and came back with a viola. Bach unfastened the buttons of his vest and tucked his violin under his chin. They all looked expectantly at Leopold.

Their guest laughed with delight and picked up his lute.

A few hours and dozens of songs later, Anna went upstairs to tuck in the children. The cantor insisted on pouring a final round of brandy for his apprentice and his guest before sending them off.

Back in his studio, he made a few more notes for the next day. Then he knelt again below the window. "As you have blessed my music, may my music bless you," he said. It was a simple prayer he repeated often, but it was sincere.

The sun had long set over the Pleisse River. He closed the shutters on the window and went out, locking the door to his studio. He was the last member of the household to turn in, snuffing out his candle on the bedside table as he crawled under the quilt. And for the few remaining hours before the rooster crowed again, Cantor Bach's pigeon coop was quiet.

<hr />

Johann Sebastian Bach was cantor and music director at St. Thomas Church in Leipzig, Germany's intellectual capital, for 27 years. As a church composer, he wrote hundreds of chorales, preludes, and fugues, as well as major works like the St. Matthew Passion *and the* Mass in B Minor. *As a musical scientist, he made great strides in the mechanics of sound, organ building, fingering, and the ergonomics of performance. Considered perhaps the world's greatest composer, he signed his compositions with the Latin phrase "Soli Deo Gloria."*

In his later years, he developed diabetes, resulting in increasing eye troubles. Two eye surgeries were unsuccessful, and he became blind for the last few months of his life. He died July 28, 1750.

Between his first wife, Maria Barbara, and his second, Anna Magdalena, J.S. Bach had 20 children, 10 of whom survived childhood. Much of what we know about his life comes from the obituary written by his son Carl Philipp Emanuel Bach, who like many of his siblings also became an accomplished musician.

THE DEVELOPMENT OF CHURCH MUSIC

EARLY AND MEDIEVAL CHURCH MUSIC: Following the practice of the Jews, the first Christians sang psalms when they gathered to worship together. The first new songs for Christian worship were written by preachers of the early church, like Ambrose of Milan (339-397), who is today known as the "Father of Western hymnody." The words of these songs usually did not quote directly from the Bible but did reflect biblical teaching.

The abbot Benedict of Nursia (480-547) in his famous "Rule," devised a cycle of eight short services for his monks to attend every few hours throughout the day. The services were designed to help the monks maintain a worshipful attitude. During these services they sang through the psalms in order, so that every week they would have sung and meditated on all 150 psalms. Today, many churches still hold Matins (daybreak), Vespers (6:00 p.m.) or Compline (evening) services in the spirit of this tradition.

As the ancient church gave way to the medieval church, it was the monks who carried on the musical expression of doctrine. One of the more famous church musicians of the Middle Ages was the abbot Bernard of Clairvaux (1090-1153). Another was Hildegard of Bingen (1098-1179), who wrote a collection of meditative songs called the "Symphonia."

Medieval church music was strictly vocal. Most theologians of the day interpreted biblical references to musical instruments as *allegorical*, meaning a physical picture of a spiritual truth. For example, they suggested that a harp was meant to signify the soul. They believed that instruments made of natural objects like wood or horse hair were too worldly to communicate the great truths of Scripture. So, with no musical accompaniment, monks sang in long, fluid phrases in a style that came to be known as *Gregorian chant*, in honor of the first medieval pope, Gregory the Great (540-604).

Most people could not read, so music was not written down. Memorizing the music sung in church helped people memorize a lot of Scripture. But some monks who had trouble remembering devised their own systems of symbols and colors, marking on paper when the tune went higher or lower. This was the beginning of modern musical notation.

Until this time, texts were sung in unison, everyone singing the same notes together, known as *monophony* (meaning "one sound"). But once people had a way to write down and read music, they found it enjoyable for a group to sing multiple melodies at the same time, known as *polyphony* (meaning "many sounds").

DEVELOPMENTS OF THE REFORMATION

Music, like preaching and Bible reading in medieval churches, was all done in Latin. The major worship service in the medieval church (beginning in the 14th century) was the *Mass*. Parts of the Mass were sung by the priests and other parts included the congregation.

A principle of the Protestant Reformers was that parts or all of a church service should be read and sung in the native language so the people can fully understand and participate. Martin Luther (1483-1546) thought German songs should be added to services in his country, so he translated some Latin musical texts into German. He then altered the traditional music to make them easier to sing or set the texts to the tunes of folk songs that people already knew. He also wrote some original hymns, including the famous "A mighty fortress is our God." Soon Lutheran songbooks were being printed for German congregations to use.

One Reformer who disagreed with Luther about music was John Calvin (1509-1564), a pastor in Geneva. Calvin understood that music has the power to move people's hearts and minds, so he wanted to be careful. He insisted on singing only texts based on the psalms, and only without instruments. In 1562, the Genevan Psalter was published after Theodore Beza (1519-1605) translated all 150 psalms into French and a professional musician named Louis Bourgeois (1510-1561) set them to music. These songs were so skillfully written that they are still sung around the world today.

In the tradition of the Lutheran songbook and Genevan Psalter, English reformers began to write and publish music for English services as well. A famous collection of music from the fifteenth and sixteenth centuries, written out with beautiful gold and colored embellishments, is the Eton Choirbook, named after Eton College where it was used.

Meanwhile, Catholic composers like Giovanni Pierluigi da Palestrina (c.1525-1594) were not to be outdone by Protestants. Some devoted their talents exclusively to writing more beautiful and complex masses.

Today most churches have a piano and do not have a pipe organ, but that is not how it was for several hundred years. The pipe organ was the most complex machine of its day, crafted by highly-skilled organ builders. Originally, the organ was used not to accompany singing but as its own contribution in certain parts of the service. By the end of the sixteenth century, Lutheran organists played during communion and provided extended introductions or preludes to the hymns.

Calvinists objected to the organ because they associated it with the Catholic service, in which the instrument took the place of some congregational singing. But Christians of other traditions believed that all musical instruments were "redeemed" by using them to glorify God. Instruments like the bassoon and cello were soon added to the musical offerings in worship.

J.S. BACH AND THE CHURCH COMPOSERS

Some of the greatest musical geniuses of all time were church composers who wrote their music specifically for the glory of God. Ahead of all his famous colleagues stands Johann Sebastian Bach (1685-1750).

By Bach's day, the Lutheran church was training and hiring musicians to participate in choirs and orchestras. Bach's role as *cantor* or music director at St. Thomas Church in Leipzig was one of the most highly respected positions in Germany. The church still used psalms and other earlier pieces, but as composers like Bach developed the art of music, the collection of worship music became wider and deeper. Bach wrote over 200 *cantatas*, or Scripture truths written as poetry and then set to music. These were sung in the church service after the gospel reading and before the sermon. He also wrote *passions*, or musical retellings of the story of Jesus' life and death, as well as organ *chorales*, or variations on a hymn tune. Nearly all Western Christians have sung Bach's lovely harmonization of Bernard of Clairvaux's hymn, "O sacred head now wounded."

Bach was the ultimate church musician, a scholar who made numerous improvements to a science that he saw as glorifying God. He was so influential that the musical era known as the *Baroque period* (1685-1750) is designated by the years of his birth and death.

Other famous composers who wrote choral (vocal) and instrumental music to be performed in church include George Frideric Handel (1685-1759), born in Germany but wrote mostly in England; the Anglican Henry Purcell (1659-1695); and the Austrian Catholic Anton Bruckner (1824-1896).

HYMN WRITING DURING THE AWAKENINGS

The era of the First and Second Great Awakenings saw a remarkable increase in the number of *hymns*, or songs written for congregational singing. A great many of these are still sung in churches today.

Perhaps the most prolific hymn writers were brothers John and Charles Wesley, both English pastors, who together wrote thousands of texts. Among these are the well-known "And can it be?" and "O for a thousand tongues to sing." John also published the Methodist hymnbook.

The Wesleys were joined by many other significant hymn writers of this period. Many were English pastors. Isaac Watts (1674-1748) wrote "When I survey the wondrous cross." Philip Doddridge (1702-1751) is remembered for his "O God of Bethel, by whose hand." Augustus M. Toplady (1740-1778) was the author of "Rock of ages."

John Newton (1725-1807), the English pastor and former slave ship captain, wrote "Amazing Grace," probably the most famous hymn of all time.

Some hymn writers were not pastors or professional theologians, but poets and teachers. The English poet William Cowper (1731-1800) wrote poems that his musician friends set to music, including "God moves in a mysterious way." Another name you will come across quite often in a hymnal is Lowell Mason (1792-1872), an American who served as organist and choir director at his Presbyterian church. He wrote over 1500 hymns in addition to teaching music in public school.

TOWARD THE MODERN PERIOD

After the Awakenings, hymn writing would continue to develop as a modern expression of worship, especially in the hands of people such as Fanny Crosby (1820-1915), Frances R. Havergal (1836-1879), and Ira D. Sankey (1840-1908). Portable organs and easy to sing melodies would become hallmarks of evangelistic tent meetings of the early twentieth century. Later decades would see the addition of pianos and guitars in church services. And Christians would keep finding new words and new tunes to sing to the Lord.

John Wesley: My Heart Strangely Warmed

JUNE 13, 1739. THE LONDON HOME OF SUSANNA WESLEY.

JOHN LEANED FORWARD in his chair and smoothed a wayward lock of hair away from his broad forehead. Though dark shadows circled his eyes, they burned with intensity as he reached the climax of his story.

"I was certain that the end was near! The ship rolled, tipping its sides into the ocean. Rivers of foaming water rushed across the deck, the wood crackling and moaning under the stress of every wave. Sailors held onto anything they could find to keep from washing overboard. 'Man your stations, men!' shouted the captain. 'Man your stations!' The words came as the ship pitched to the left. The ocean reared its rolling head, looking for someone to wash out to sea, and then withdrew, leaving a few fish flopping on the slippery deck. 'We're going to die!' someone screamed. A violent shock against the bow of the ship brought it to a sudden stop, knocking passengers about, their bleeding arms and legs twisting in a jumbled mess. Another bolt of lightning, and someone managed to light a lamp. I had a boot in my face, with a man attached to it! We picked ourselves up, and waited for the final blow."

The small woman interrupted him with an offer of tea.

"Mother!" he exclaimed. "I'm in the middle of telling my story."

"Yes," she nodded, "and such a story requires tea. If my son is going to be accused of having gone mad, my nerves must be fortified with a strong cup of tea."

"I'm not insane," insisted John, squaring his shoulders against the back of the chair. "Quite the opposite. I only now understand what it means to truly trust in Christ."

Susanna poured the steaming, fragrant liquid into two delicate cups and picked up the one closest to her. "But I am concerned, my son," she said after blowing across the surface and taking a sip. "Your brother, Samuel, tells me that Mrs. Hutton complained to him last June that you disrupted her home with a bunch of nonsense about not being a Christian. He sent me this."

She pulled a folded slip of paper from the pocket of her dress and handed it to him across the tea tray.

John smoothed out the creases and shrugged. "Yes, Mother, this is my written testimony. I read it to you last year. You were not concerned about it then."

"But now I'm reading it again in light of the incident at the Huttons, and I worry that you have left the church for some heresy."

"Mrs. Hutton exaggerates." He stood up abruptly and paced the room, brushing absently at his black overcoat. They were in her parlor, a small rectangle with a fireplace on one wall, a narrow window on another wall, and doorways on the remaining two sides. His pacing was limited since he could cross the room in just a few steps.

"I don't know Mrs. Hutton, but I certainly hope she has overstated this incident. A man in his mid thirties—especially a man I raised—ought not disrupt the homes of others." She picked up his tea cup and held it out to him.

He stopped pacing and looked into her wide recessive eyes. She nodded at the upholstered chair facing hers. He took the cup and returned to his seat.

"I need to hear the full story from you, my son."

He drained his cup all at once and set it back on the tray with a clink of china. "Mother, you taught our family theology. You brought us up so we could tell right from wrong, did you not?"

"Yes, I did," she said proudly.

"Then you trust me?"

"Trusting you to do what you think is right, and trusting you to do what is actually right are two different things," she said, sipping again from her cup. "Continue with your story."

He took up his storyteller's pose again. "As I was saying, the ship was tossed back and forth until we all wondered if we were going to die—."

"Yes." She waved her hand. "I've got that part."

"Amidst all the chaos, I saw some Moravian Christians praying quietly. They were holding on to the benches to keep from sliding around, but they appeared unafraid to die. I was not so sure about myself. I asked if they were afraid of death, and one of the ministers said that none of them, not even the children, were afraid. They were convinced of their status before God. They began to sing and pray. I joined in. Above decks, the storm raged so violently that the mainsail was ripped in pieces. But down below as I sat through the storm with the Moravians, I enjoyed a calmness brought on only by trusting in God. That calmness was, in a way, startling."

He took a deep breath. "The storm passed and the ship docked safely. But when we arrived at the Savannah settlement in the Georgia territory, things began to change. Mr. James Oglethorpe..."

Susanna interrupted again. "He is the governor of the Georgia territory?"

"Yes. The one Charles told you about."

She frowned. "The man who disliked your brother and made it difficult for him to live in America."

"That is the one. He introduced me to a very odd Moravian minister named Spangenberg. I had barely begun to speak to the man when he asked me the question."

"You mean, a question."

"No," said John, "I mean *the* question. Before Charles and I left, I told him that though I came to America to convert the Indians, I was hoping to be converted myself. Spangenberg looked at me and asked, 'Do you know Christ?'"

"And you said yes."

"No, I didn't," John exclaimed. "I blinked. That was all I could do at first, blink. And then he asked me again."

"Well, of course you know Christ. You're a minister. I taught you about the Lord and you participated in baptism and the Eucharist." She set down her cup. "That is lovely tea. I must remember where I purchased it."

"But I didn't feel as if I knew Christ!" John cried. "I needed evidence."

She shook her head. "What evidence do you need, my son? You have the promises of the sacraments themselves."

"But if I were in a relationship with Christ, shouldn't there be something inside of me, a feeling of assurance?" He was leaning forward again, his palms pressed against his knees.

"Feelings are deceitful. You know that well."

John stared at the window.

"It was your feelings, after all, that got you in trouble in America."

He nodded. "Yes, but that was different."

"Different because it involved a girl?"

"Different because it was before my recent conversion."

She gave him a penetrating look. "I do not understand how you and Charles could be in America for so little time and yet make so many enemies."

He threw his hands in the air. "Charles didn't want to go in the first place. He was the victim. He was led to believe that Oglethorpe did some unsavory things. So he brought up accusations against Oglethorpe, only to find out too late that they were false. After that, Oglethorpe made life difficult for Charles. He had promised Charles he could live in his mansion in Frederica, but after their public disagreement, he refused to even furnish the house. Charles slept on a hard floor in a bare room. It was very depressing. And you know how temperamental musicians can be!"

"Apparently as temperamental as ministers," she murmured.

"Well, I was at least able to heal the rift between the two men," said John. "It was too bad that Charles wouldn't stay. I could have used his help."

"Yes, apparently you aren't as good at fixing your own problems."

"Mother, you know it wasn't as simple as that," he insisted. "When I arrived, I planned to be a minister to the Indians, but I ended up being vicar of Savannah. Politics being what they are, I was hardly off to a good start. I became the leader of the Savannah Society, which, like our groups here in England, met to reprove and exhort one another in the faith. But despite this, I was never completely accepted by the colony."

She turned her steady gaze on him again. "Are you going to tell me how you met Miss Hopkey?"

John was uncomfortable discussing this with his mother, so he poured a second cup of tea before he answered. "I was teaching at the school in Savannah. She was eighteen years old at the time."

"Your brother tells me she nursed you to health when you were sick."

"She did," said John, turning towards the window. "She even read me prayers and cooked."

"She sounds like a lovely girl. Charles says you told her that you would be happy if she would marry you."

"Yes."

"But then you left her." Her eyes narrowed. "You led her to believe you were in love with her!"

"I was!"

"What would cause a son of mine to treat a young lady so shamefully?"

He jumped up again and carried his cup toward the window. "I thought marriage would interfere with my dedication to the church. That's why I broke it off. Anyway, I later discovered that she was no longer waiting for me, but was to be married to Mr. Williamson."

Susanna did not reply.

He turned to face her. "I had the best of intentions, Mother. I was determined to reject the things of this world."

"Yes, I still have the letter you sent me saying you were going to forsake the world for the cause of the church. But that does not explain why, when Miss Hopkey decided to marry Mr. Williamson, you forbade her and her husband from receiving communion."

"They did not publish an announcement of their wedding. It is a requirement of the church, to allow for a public objection if such is necessary. Since they went against the regulations of the church, they were put under discipline. I could not allow them to take communion."

"You never excused other couples who did the same?"

He fidgeted with his high collar. "I may not have been consistent all the time. But it was my duty to hold them accountable."

"I'm just reminding you how feelings or experiences can sometimes cloud our vision. You allowed jealousy to get in the way of your pastoral responsibilities, and her uncle accused you of abusing your office. There are consequences to our actions."

"I know! That is why I had to flee America and return to

England. But it has turned out to be a good thing."

"What do you mean?"

"When one's heart is not content, one searches for answers."

Her brow wrinkled with hesitation. "That is true, but—."

"And I found what I was looking for!" He took his chair across from her again. "When I was in Savannah, I was beating the air, as they say. I was ignorant of the righteousness of Christ. I was continually fighting my sin, but never conquering it. I did not have the Spirit of Christ testifying with my spirit, so that I could rest in the knowledge that Christ had died for me. I was still looking for freedom."

He reached across the tea tray and took her hand. It was soft and cold. He buried it between both of his to warm her. The weight of his journal in his chest pocket urged him to go on with his story.

"Since my return to England I had kept up a conversation with Mr. Peter Bohler. He encouraged me to look deep into my heart and to know whether I truly trust in Christ. Peter is a pious and gentle man, and loved by everyone. He consistently pointed me to Christ. One afternoon, Peter told me that there are two fruits of faith, dominion over sin and a sense of forgiveness. I had neither, so I continued to seek faith."

"And?"

"And on May 24, last year—sometime in the morning—I opened my Bible and read 2 Peter 1:4, which told me to be a partaker of the divine nature." He was looking out the window again. "That day I went to St. Paul's Cathedral. I remember walking up to its pillars and wondering if my heart was as dead as some of the others who attended the church. They sang an anthem that seemed to be directed at my emptiness. I still remember the words:

Out of the deep have I called unto thee, O Lord: Lord hear my voice. O let thine ears consider well the voice of my complaint. If thou, Lord, wilt be extreme to mark what is done amiss, O Lord, who may abide it? But there is mercy with thee; therefore thou shalt be feared. O Israel, trust in the Lord: For with the Lord is mercy, and with him is plenteous redemption. And he shall redeem Israel from all his sins.

"That night I was asked to go to a meeting of a Methodist society on Aldersgate Street. A man was reading Martin Luther's preface to the book of Romans. It was just a few minutes before nine, and while he was describing the change that God performs in the heart of the person through faith in Christ, I—." John paused.

"Yes?" his mother urged.

He looked her in the eye. "I felt my heart strangely warmed. I had an assurance in my soul by the Holy Spirit that I did trust Christ, and Christ alone, for my salvation. I had an assurance that Christ has indeed taken away even my sins."

"But my son—you didn't have this before?"

He shook his head.

She withdrew her hands and tucked them in the ends of her shawl, leaning back thoughtfully.

"I began to read about other Christians who had similar experiences," John continued. "I read Thomas à Kempis, who spoke about true Christianity as an intimate relationship with Christ. I read Jonathan Edwards's *Faithful Narrative of the Surprising Work of God* and discovered that the Spirit does do marvelous works in the souls of human beings. He did so at Edwards's church in Northampton only a few years ago."

"I raised you to look for the evidence of God in your life," said his mother. "You are telling me that you never saw this evidence in your own heart before your Aldersgate experience?"

"I never did," insisted John. "That night was the first time in my life I had truly experienced conversion. Everything before that was a delusion."

"Well, what about Mrs. Hutton?" Susanna said, touching the letter from Charles still on the tray before her. "She insists that you are crazy. Why does she believe this?"

"Mr. and Mrs. Hutton were kind enough to let me stay with them. A few days after the Aldersgate meeting, while Mr. Hutton was reading a sermon to a group of us, I couldn't hold in my exciting news any longer. I blurted out that not five days before I had been an unbeliever."

"I'm sure they found your behavior very odd. Not to mention rude, in the middle of a sermon."

"Yes, of course. The outburst was badly timed. But Mrs. Hutton was incensed. She said that if I wasn't a Christian before then, I was the best hypocrite she knew."

Susanna chuckled. "I was thinking something similar myself! You certainly acted like a Christian before that ... most of the time." She was thinking of Miss Hopkey, but did not mention her.

"I didn't know I was a hypocrite until I finally came to faith. Anyway, I think Mrs. Hutton was worried that I would be a bad influence on her sons, who look up to me. She feared that I was going to challenge the sacraments of the church, that I was going to reject my baptism."

"Do you?" she demanded.

"No. I remain well within the bounds of the Church of England," he assured her. "The difference is that now I am certain of my salvation."

Susanna stood and went toward the bookshelf. That corner of the room was drafty, and she wrapped her shawl tighter to her body. Opening a small box on the shelf, she took out another letter. She unfolded it and read aloud. "Long my imprisoned spirit lay, fast bound in sin and nature's night. Thine eye diffused a quickening ray; I woke, the dungeon flamed with light. My chains fell off, my heart was free, I rose, went forth, and followed thee."

"Yes! That's what happened to me." John looked at her intently, his eyes lit up again. "Those words sound familiar."

"They should," she replied. "It is a hymn your brother, Charles, wrote recently."

"Yes. It is based on his own conversion experience, similar to mine."

She nodded and kept reading. "No condemnation now I dread; Jesus, and all in him, is mine; alive in him, my living Head, and clothed in righteousness divine, bold I approach the eternal throne, and claim the crown, through Christ my own."

Susanna tucked the letter back in the box. Then she went to her son and took his head in her hands. "If this is the experience you had, then only those that do not truly know Christ will think you crazy."

He took her hands from his face and kissed them. "That is just how I would describe what happened to me, Mother."

She smiled. "Then I shall have no further problem with what I hear about you," she said. "To know Christ in this way is a desirable thing. And I know that God has called you to do something great for him." She sat down again. "You know, I have a story of my own to tell you."

He groaned. "Not the fire again!"

"Yes, the fire story." She raised her chin. "And you hold your tongue while I tell it."

He winked and put a finger across his lips.

"You were just a boy," she said, half-closing her eyes to remember. "Your father was the minister of Epworth. One night the rectory caught on fire. It was between eleven and twelve at night when the roof went up in flames. We were all asleep, unaware of the danger spreading over us! Until your father shook me awake. I was with child, and the smoke was disorienting. Neighbors were shouting, helping us escape through the garden door. But it wasn't until we were on the other side of the flames and I was counting and kissing my beautiful children's heads that I realized one of you had been left behind."

She opened her eyes and fixed them on John. "It was you, my

son. I feared you were already dead. Your father tried to enter the house again, but the flames pushed him back. And then we saw your head poking out an upstairs window, shouting and sobbing. The roof above you was nearly consumed! But your father and the neighbor managed to climb up the side of the house that was still standing and yank you out the window. You all fell back to the ground just as the roof collapsed on your bedroom."

"I knew that night that God had spared you for a special calling, John. When you left for America, I wondered if that calling was to evangelize the Indians. And then when you snuck back to England in disgrace, I sorrowed at how you had run away like the prophet Jonah! But now, now I see he had been preparing your soul to be sensitive to his spirit. This is only the beginning of your work, John. You must persevere in your faith. I trust that the Lord will have mercy on this mother and let her see the great work he will do in her son."

He looked at her, the corners of his mouth twitching. "May I speak now?"

"My preacher son pretends he can keep silent! What do you think of my story?"

He stood and kissed the top of her head. "Thank you, Mother. For teaching me about Christ, and for living for him in my presence. And for believing in your wayward son." He fastened the large pewter buttons on his overcoat. "Come on. Walk with me as far as the garden. I'll clear the tea things for you."

With a smile, she tightened her shawl across her shoulders and followed her son out to the kitchen.

John Wesley went on to be the leader of the Methodist movement and an important figure in the First Great Awakening in England. He preached to thousands of people and his teachings have influenced generations of Christians. Wesley's belief that the Christian life must be a living and

active faith encouraged many Christians to serve the poor and free slaves. His brother, Charles, wrote some of the most important hymns of the church, a good number of which are sung all over the world.

Susanna Wesley died just a few years after this conversation in 1742. John died in 1791.

An Era of Social Reform

IF THE GOSPEL is the heart of Christianity, charity is its hands. When Jesus was asked which commandment was the most important, he replied: "Love the Lord your God with all your heart and with all your soul and with all your mind and with all your strength. The second is this: 'Love your neighbor as yourself.' There is no commandment greater than these" (Mark 12:30-31 NIV).

During the time of the Great Awakenings, Evangelical Christians called for a renewed commitment to these commandments. To truly love God, they argued, is to be willing to love your neighbor as yourself. They emphasized the active Christian life in evangelism, missions, and social action.

SLAVERY

The most obvious area of social action was the issue of slavery. It is hard for us to understand now, but for thousands of years slavery was an everyday part of human existence. Many people—including many Christians—believed that slave labor was necessary for the world to function. They argued that the Bible regulates slavery, but does not condemn it.

Christians differed from each other about the reasons for engaging in slavery and what forms were permitted. For example, Jonathan Edwards owned several slaves at one time or another. He treated them kindly, and he spoke out against the Atlantic slave trade, believing it hurt missions. He also believed that only war captives, debtors, and children of slaves—not free persons—could be purchased legitimately as slaves. And he admitted slaves into membership at his church, a remarkable thing at the time. But he still accepted that some people could be owned by other people. Revivalist George Whitfield also owned slaves and even petitioned Parliament for the legalization of slavery in Georgia, because he needed workers for his orphanage! But at the same time, he also preached against their cruel treatment.

If Christians in the eighteenth and nineteenth centuries defended slavery as a way of life, what led them to change their minds?

ABOLITIONISM

In England, John Wesley and other Evangelical Methodists preached against the slave trade, believing it to be contrary to the gospel. They influenced statesmen like William Wilberforce (1759-1833), who with William Pitt (1759-1806), Granville Sharp (1735-1813), Thomas Clarkson (1760-1846), Olaudah Equiano (c.1745-1797), and other abolitionists led a brilliant political campaign to abolish the slave trade in Britain. Most British citizens had never personally been exposed to the horrors of slavery, since the slaves went straight to the West Indies plantations and not to the streets of London. But when Wilberforce and his colleagues publicized the deathly conditions the slaves faced, they successfully changed the official policies of an entire nation.

In North America, as the black slave population grew, so did the number of black ministers and revivalists. Some of the white Evangelicals who worked with their black brothers became convinced of the abolitionist cause. Samuel Hopkins (1721-1803), a student of Jonathan Edwards, applied the writings of his teacher to make an argument against slavery. Presbyterian pastor Lyman Beecher (1775-1863) also opposed slavery, as did his daughter, author Harriet Beecher Stowe (1811-1896), who wrote novels about slave life to help people understand. Sojourner Truth (c.1797-1883) was a runaway slave who was given shelter and the gospel by a group of Methodists. Though she could not read or write, she became an influential leader, traveling from town to town telling others about the sin of slavery. Some slaves like Sojourner published slave narratives, telling their stories to make others aware of life as a slave. These Christians from all backgrounds became leaders calling for change. Slavery was one of the many issues of the American Civil War, when it was finally outlawed in all of the States.

OTHER REFORMS AROUND THE WORLD

The end of slavery was only one of many social improvements championed by Christians during the First and Second Great Awakenings. Elizabeth Fry (1780-1845), a British Quaker, was a tireless justice fighter who convinced her government to give fair treatment to prisoners. She argued for the end of the death penalty, especially since at that time people were executed for any number of minor offenses. She helped prisoners start schools and sewing businesses in the prisons. And instead of putting mentally ill people in jail, as most countries did then, she set up hospitals where these people—made in the image of God!—could get better treatment. Her ideas were later implemented in other countries, including Russia.

Evangelicals also began to establish foreign mission agencies. Many believed that offering the gospel to people also meant giving clothes to the poor, feeding the hungry, and educating those who did not have access to schools. These were tangible ways to show their love for the people to whom they ministered. British missionary William Carey (1761-1834), for example, preached the gospel in India. But he also tried to end the unjust caste system and eliminate inhumane practices like *sati*, in which widows were burned with their husband's bodies. American missionary Fidelia Fiske (1816-1864) took the gospel to Iran and there became a protector of abused girls.

So the First and Second Great Awakenings were the historical beginnings of Evangelical action. Christians outside of Evangelical traditions were also contributing. For example, Roman Catholic missionaries were building schools and hospitals around the world, too. But it was Evangelicals who most often pointed to the connection between believing and acting, between heart and hands. To love God means obeying his command to love our neighbors, and Evangelicals of the Awakenings were doing this in a big way.

WILLIAM WILBERFORCE AND THE ABOLITIONISTS: GREAT CHANGE

SPRING 1788. THE PORT OF LIVERPOOL, ENGLAND.

THE SHARP SCENT of salt tingled in his nostrils. He was glad for the cloudy night that cloaked him from the sailors' eyes. Most of them had gone ashore to the taverns, but a few remained to man the ship at port. The wind off the water was just loud enough to hide the sounds of his movements as he crept closer to the deck. On the starboard side of the ship, several sailors tipped their glasses together, unaware that he was joining them in the darkness.

He was getting used to the fear of being caught. For weeks, the man known to England as Thomas Clarkson, abolitionist, rode his horse furiously from sea port to sea port. Parliament had agreed to investigate the slave trade, and Thomas and his friends knew the slave traders would be trying to get rid of the evidence on their ships. So he needed to collect it. Quietly and quickly.

The deck creaked with every step, but Thomas kept going until he reached the doorway leading to the lower decks. Flickers of candlelight lit the stairs. He climbed down until he had reached the bowels of the ship, then grabbed an oil lamp and turned up the flame. The yellow light exposed hundreds of rows of wooden planks, just wide enough for a man to lie down on.

As he crept forward, the lamplight reflected off metal shackles attached to the sides of the planks. They were stained with blood, clearly the bonds of a slave. It was obvious to Thomas that the ship was designed to haul large numbers of immobile captives across the ocean. The planks were just far enough apart to fit a slave with barely enough room to breathe.

"Those poor men would have to lie still on these planks for weeks or months," he thought, imagining the cramps in his arms and legs.

He tried to remove one of the shackles from a plank, but it wouldn't budge. "I already have one of these anyway," he thought. "This time I'm looking for something else."

He kept moving through the hull toward a small room. Along the wall he found a shelf of boxes. He was about to riffle through them when he heard approaching voices. He quickly turned down his lamp, hung it on a hook, and pressed himself into the corner.

Two men passed him.

"This was a profitable trip," said one. "We only lost a quarter of our cargo."

"Disappointed the sharks, eh?" said the other.

"When we toss the dead slaves overboard, those sharks follow us for miles!"

Thomas burned with anger. "You're talking about human beings!" he thought. He clenched his fist, tempted to show the sailors how it felt to be tossed overboard. But he resisted the urge. When the men had gone above, he picked up his lamp again and proceeded to go through the boxes.

"Here's what I was looking for," he soon muttered. In his hands was a steel clamp contraption, used to force-feed slaves when they refused to eat on the way to England. He stuffed the device in the leather bag on his shoulder, hung the lamp back on the wall, and quickly ascended the stairs.

As he neared the opening to the deck, a shadowy figure passed in front of it. Thomas shrank back. The shadow hesitated in front of the doorway as though it was peering straight down at him. Thomas didn't breathe, hoping his brown coat blended in with the gloom. But the figure began to descend toward him.

He had only two options. He could try to sneak back down the stairs, but then he would be trapped there. Or he could just make a break for it and knock down the person, but he wasn't sure he could outrun the sailors on the deck. "Quick, think of an excuse for being here!" he urged himself.

The figure was almost upon him when a shaft of moonlight exposed the face.

"Equiano?" Thomas whispered in relief.

His partner put a hand on his shoulder. "You've taken too long, my friend. I was worried you had been caught."

"I'm glad it's you," said Thomas, nudging his friend back up the stairs. "But we must get out of here immediately. The sailors will not abide an African thief on their slave ship!"

Equiano gave him a sidelong glance. "How sad for them to have their instruments of terror stolen!"

Carefully, the two men slipped passed the drunken sailors and down the dock. They didn't speak again until they reached the spot where Equiano had hidden their horses.

Thomas lifted his bag. "Do you want to see what I took?"

Equiano looked him in the eye. "Whatever you have found on that evil ship, I have already seen it and do not want to see again."

"Of course," Thomas hurried to say. "I'm sorry, my friend." He quickly tucked the satchel into his saddle bags.

"But I am grateful you found what you needed," Equiano said. "Wilberforce and the others will be glad for the evidence we've collected."

"Then let us deliver it safely," said Thomas, and he urged his horse forward.

In a house in London, a man shivered and tossed on his sweat-soaked sheets. "Water," he moaned, clutching both hands to his stomach.

The exasperated doctor turned to the elegant young man hovering nearby. "Help me hold him still," he said. He turned to his patient and chided, "You must stop moving, Mr. Wilberforce! I need to listen to your heart."

As soon as the doctor had finished his ministrations, the man began to question him anxiously. "Will he recover?"

"I cannot say, Mr. Prime Minister. My diagnosis remains the same. He has decay of the digestive tracts."

"Can you do nothing more for him?"

The doctor hesitated. "There is a drug I can give him which may help a little. But too much will produce other difficulties, Mr. Pitt, and—."

At 29, the Prime Minister was young—in fact, the youngest England had ever had—but he carried himself with the dignity of the office. "Dr. Warren," he said now with quiet authority. "William Wilberforce is a Member of Parliament and a dear friend. I need him to get better and finish our work. If this treatment will help, he must have it."

The doctor threw up his hands. "He will need to go to the city of Bath for supervised treatment."

"Very well," said Pitt. "I will make the arrangements."

William mumbled in his bed.

"What was that?" Pitt said, rushing to his side. "I think he said 'oak tree.'"

"It's the fever," insisted the doctor. "Let's give him time to rest. This has been a bad episode."

Pitt stood looking over his friend as the doctor left the room. "No," he said to himself. "It's not the fever. It's his reason to live."

He knew William was thinking of a particular sprawling oak tree on Pitt's estate in Holwood. The two friends had once sat down to rest under its protective branches. They had been discussing the great evil of the slave trade, the buying and selling of human beings. The idea of English businessmen forcing their African brothers to labor to death on sugar plantations in the West Indies made their stomachs turn!

But for William, so did the idea of risking his career for the slaves' cause. Like his friend Pitt, William was smart and ambitious, and despite his youth had already risen to a prestigious seat in Parliament. Slavery was just the way the world operated. Somebody had to do the back-breaking work, right? Most people believed that God created some to rule and the rest to serve the rulers. It would be nearly impossible to convince England to abolish slavery. Must he throw away his future for such a lost cause?

"Is it a lost cause or a just cause, Wilberforce?" Pitt had demanded. "Great change must come or we remain slaves to our own lusts."

"Great change," William had repeated. The words meant a lot to him. He had used them to describe his conversion to Christianity a few years earlier. At the time, he thought becoming a serious Christian meant he would have to give up politics and do "the Lord's work" instead. His friend John Newton, the old former slave ship captain who now wrote poetry, insisted that Parliament was just the place for God to use William's "salt and light." Pitt agreed, reminding William that Christian principles lead not just to meditation but also to action. Well, he had taken their advice then and stayed in politics. But how much "great change" could one man endure?

William had flung his hat down on one of the rambling roots of the oak and sighed. "Slavery has been on my mind constantly," he admitted. "I do not know how a nation that claims to be Christian can remain in the abhorrent act of trading other human beings."

Pitt gave him a hard look. "The day is coming, William, when someone will step up to take on the slave traders. The only question is, will it be you?"

He knew from the look on William's gentle face that the answer was yes.

Not long after, Thomas Clarkson had showed up at William's door, dumping evidence of the terrors of slave ships on his table. Each instrument of torture and brutality had burned into their memories. With their friend Granville Sharpe as the chairman, the men formed a group they called the Clapham Sect because they met at William's house in the London suburb of Clapham. Their purpose was to fight the traders in the British courts. William became their spokesperson. He had a way of talking to people that won them over to his point of view.

Standing over his friend now, watching William struggle with his illness, Pitt thought it was time for another speech. "William, you must pull yourself out of this," he demanded. "You have work to do. Your friends Newton and Wesley and others all insist that God has called you to this cause. Your nation—no, the human nation—needs you to do this!"

In his fever, William didn't respond.

Pitt sank to the chair at his friend's bedside to wait. Hours later, he was dozing when he heard William's moan change into a whisper.

"Ah, you're awake again!"

William's eyelids fluttered. He looked up at Pitt, his face colorless except for the dark smudges below his blue eyes, and smiled weakly. "Why are you letting me lie here, Pitt? You need me in the Commons."

"Yes I do," Pitt agreed with a grin. But he quickly grew serious again as William winced with pain. "However, you are not ready to return."

His slim hands trembling, William drew his shirt closed and

tried to smooth out the wrinkles. "We can't let the issue fall to the wayside," he began.

"We can't let you fall to the wayside either. You are going to Bath for treatment."

William shook his fair head. "No, I'm going back to Parliament."

"You are not going to convince anyone of the cause if you are vomiting all over the House."

"But we need to make a resolution——."

"Yes. I am supervising the Privy Council's investigation into the trade and Thomas has returned with several important pieces of evidence. I plan to make a resolution in your absence on the ninth of May."

William opened his mouth to reply, but was again interrupted, this time by a knock at the door. Pitt opened it to find Thomas Clarkson.

"Wilberforce!" cried Thomas. "You must be so good for nothing that even death doesn't want you."

From his pillow, William gave him a good-natured groan. "Apparently you are not as particular about your friends."

"I am not," agreed Thomas, dropping into the chair by the bed. "Why, I even count the Prime Minister here a friend."

Pitt laughed. "For my part, I have publicly and repeatedly disavowed any association with you."

Thomas wagged his eyebrows at William. "Politics! Well, William, you and I are clearly survivors. The traders have put a mark on my head and your delicate stomach has put a mark on this sick room. I believe death is even less successful than Parliament!"

"Enough of your amusements at my expense," said Pitt, crossing his arms. "How has your, ah, 'fact finding mission' gone so far?"

"I suppose 'illuminating' is the right word. And 'sickening.' I can't tell you how many sailors I have interviewed. And I have built a repulsive collection of objects that I certainly hope someone else will take custody of soon. But I fear first I will have to explain how each item works."

William nodded. "The least we can do for our brothers is understand what they have been forced to suffer."

"Agreed." Pitt nudged Thomas toward the door. "For now, I need to get back to my office to prepare for the next resolution, and William needs to rest. We'll need his charm and wit if we are ever to succeed."

As soon as William was well enough to travel, he went to Bath for medical treatment. From there he kept up correspondence with French officials he was encouraging to outlaw the trade in France. William and his colleagues knew it was important to spread the abolition movement to other countries, too. If they were ever successful in ending this crime in Britain, they didn't want the traders to be able to just move their operations somewhere else.

Meanwhile, the young Prime Minister was occupied with the business of the country. On the ninth of May, as he promised William, he made a resolution in the House of Commons to "take into consideration the issue of slave trade, which many have complained about and petitioned for change." With those words, he had opened the door to a great debate.

Later, he was happy to report to William that a first step had been taken. During the following session of Parliament, one of the Members, Mr. Dolben, proposed a limit on the number of slaves that could be transported on one ship.

"That is hardly an improvement!" protested William.

"I know it is not much, but fresh air and more room to breathe is better than the previous conditions," Pitt argued. "And you should have heard the objections that were raised to just this minor change! But I have hope, William. Dolben isn't the only one questioning the morality of the trade. We are gaining support. I'll send you the report of the Privy Council as soon as I get it."

Spring had come around again by the time William had

sufficiently recovered from his severe illness. Back in his study at home, windows open to let in the sound of the breeze among the birch trees, he leaned over a table piled with papers. He was trying to memorize the 850-page report of the council when his friends arrived. By now, they had changed the name of their Clapham Sect to the Society for the Abolition of the Slave Trade.

Thomas had brought a heavy chest filled with evidence from the slave ships. He left it in front of the wall of books and waved an inventory list at the men around the table. "Equiano and I have ridden about 35,000 miles to get these materials. My back will never be the same, but when William presents these in the House, my labor will be worth it."

"Dolben's Act was a small victory," said Pitt. "When he argued for regulating the trade, the trade sympathizers claimed that the slaves have plenty of room on their ships. They even had the nerve to bring in some sailors to testify that the slaves were happy on the ship, that they thanked them for rescuing them!"

"For a price, you can get any testimony," declared Granville Sharpe.

"But that claim will be impossible to substantiate," said William.

"Especially once this is made public," said Equiano, holding up a long wooden box. When he flipped open the latch and tapped on the base, a large roll of paper slid onto the table.

William unrolled the document. He stared at it for a moment before he realized what he was looking at. It was a sketch of a ship from various angles. At first he thought the many rows of small figures were letters of a foreign language, but then he realized they were people packed like a tin of sardines. It was just as Dolben had claimed in his motion to Parliament. Men, women, and children chained together on planks with few air holes, no toilet, no room to move.

"There is a mere forty centimeters between planks," Equiano

said quietly. "This is how they spend their weeks or months at the bottom of the ship, unless they die on the way."

William squeezed his eyes shut and swallowed hard, trying to keep down his dinner.

"This is the plan of the ship known as the *Brookes*, named after the Brookes family of shipping merchants," Thomas explained, tapping a finger on the paper. "It is also similar to the design of the *Liverpool*. The plan shows room for 454 slaves, but prior to Dolben's Act, the traders would pack 600 people on this ship."

William rolled up the page and pushed it back across the table to Equiano. "If the British people see this, they will not believe the lies of the traders," he said.

"It has already been presented to the House of Commons," noted Pitt.

"We must do more than that," insisted William. "We need a massive campaign to raise the awareness of the people."

"Indeed," said Thomas. "That is why I've arranged for a publisher to print this. We're going to circulate as many copies on the street as we can."

"There is also this." Equiano handed a stack of pages to William.

"What is it?" Granville asked from the other side of the table.

"My book," said Equiano, his dark face beaming.

William read the cover page aloud. "The Interesting Narrative of the Life of Olaudah Equiano." He looked up, his eyes sparked with enthusiasm. "Do you already have a publisher?"

"Yes. It is my hope that each Member of Parliament will read it and learn what I and so many others suffered."

"Excellent work," said Granville, reaching out to shake his hand. "And has anyone heard from Josiah Wedgwood?"

"I have," said Pitt. "He's offered to design one of his beautiful ceramic pieces with the image of a slave and the words 'Am I not a man and a brother?' He plans to put it on tobacco boxes and brooches so aristocrats can show their friends they support our cause."

"Wonderful!"

"Well, gentlemen, it looks like our campaign has begun!" William rose, his cheeks and lips pink with excitement. "I will soon be making a speech before the House of Commons. If I can convince the other Members of what we already know, we may be able to take abolition to the next step!"

The men looked at each other across the table, hope radiating from their faces.

William put a hand on the stacks of the council's report. "I need to finish going through all this information to prepare my speech. And I think we should commission someone to build a model of the ship in that sketch. I want my colleagues to see that sea-dungeon with their own eyes."

"I know someone," said Pitt.

"Good. And Thomas, I don't really want to know what all the pieces in your collection are for, but I'm afraid it is the only way I can fully understand the slaves' plight. Can you stay behind and explain the evidence to me?"

"Of course."

The other men left William and Thomas to their unpleasant research. Later, after Thomas left, William went back to reading the report. Every day for the next several weeks, he pored over the pages, consuming the details and shaping his speech until he knew exactly what he was going to say. How he said it would be as important as what he said. He knew his words before the House of Commons had the potential to end British slavery.

The morning of Tuesday, May 12, William woke with a stomachache. He didn't know if it was his ongoing illness or his nerves, but he was determined to present his case. "Great change," he reminded himself as he got out of bed. "When I became a Christian, the works of Philip Doddridge and John Wesley showed me that I must give my life to Christ. Despite my many infirmities, with God's help I will serve him for however long he gives me."

He took his medicine and then, slipping on his dressing gown, went to his study to go over his notes again.

A few hours later, William joined his colleagues in the House of Commons at the Palace of Westminster. The chamber had the look of a chapel, with a small platform in the middle surrounded by rows of benches. Pitt, as Prime Minister, sat in the center of the floor behind a table where clerks recorded the business. The Members of Parliament, young men and old men, in top hats and vests and riding boots, sat on either side. It was each man's job to represent his district in the governing body of England.

Pitt called the session to order. When the time came for his address, William rose from his spot on the bench and faced his fellow lawmakers with sober eyes.

"When I consider the magnitude of the subject which I am to bring before the House—a subject which interests the whole world—it is impossible for me not to feel terrified and concerned at my own inadequacy for such a task." He looked at the floor and slowly raised his arms. "I, with the whole of Parliament and Great Britain, am shamed for allowing this horrid trade to continue under our authority."

A murmur swept the hall. He knew some of the Members would object, but what he said was true.

"Let him speak!" someone shouted.

He cleared his throat and continued. "Imagine 600 or 700 slaves chained two-by-two, surrounded by disease and other wretchedness! One man connected to another by the ankle, and if they resisted, their wrists bound. How can we bear the thought?"

He presented the model ship, and held it up so they could all see how the slaves would be packed inside.

"This House has heard previous testimony that the slaves are joyful at their capture, that they are grateful to be locked away and carried off to a strange land to break their backs. What a lie! Today I will give you the true facts, with evidence. For instance, the poor slaves are so miserable that the slave captains often set sail at night to make it harder for them to escape. On average, twelve percent of these people die on the journey. Another fifty percent die from mistreatment after they arrive! And many of the sailors forced to participate in these odious deeds die from disease, too."

The Members shifted on their seats. Some looked angry. Some looked shocked. But at least they were all reacting.

William knew he had their attention now. "I'm afraid I have many more repulsive details to tell you," he said. He moved through his arguments carefully. He gave them a summary of the Privy Council's report. He described the evidence Thomas and Equiano had collected. He quoted the testimony of slaves who had survived the horrors.

His speech continued for three and a half hours. Before he finished, he turned and faced the Prime Minister, his friend Pitt, squarely. "Sir, when we think of eternity, and of the future consequences of our conduct, what can make any man contradict his conscience, the principles of justice, the laws of religion, and even God himself?" He was standing on tiptoe now, his voice passionate. "A trade founded on such iniquity must be abolished, whatever the consequences. I will never rest until it is abolished!"

An uproar filled the hall as the Members jumped up from their benches. The House was one place you would always find a good shouting match! William saw angry fists in the air. But many of his colleagues were on their feet cheering for him.

A great debate began. Before it was over, several supporters of the trade moved to postpone any decisions until they could present evidence for their side. To William's surprise, the Members agreed. Deflated, he rode to Pitt's country estate at the end of the day.

"It was a fantastic speech, William," Pitt insisted when he joined him in the parlor. "Everyone is praising it."

But William threw himself across the velvet sofa and shook his head. "Given the evidence already before the House, I can't believe the trade supporters think they can defend it." He sighed. "I've been too optimistic about how fast we can do this."

Pitt dropped a gentle hand on his friend's shoulder. "Change of this magnitude cannot happen overnight. But if we push forward, it can happen in our lifetimes."

William didn't respond. He was running through his speech in his head, wondering what he could have said differently to convince them.

But soon Thomas burst into the room, shouting. "Did you see it? Have you heard?"

William sat up. "What is it?"

Thomas waved a newspaper above his head. "The papers are calling your speech a triumph, and a deathnell for the slave merchants of Liverpool. 'The African bonds of bolts and chains are no more!' the report says. Look here!" He threw the paper in William's lap.

William scanned the paper with a changed face. "This means public opinion is now on our side! The people of Britain have come to see this horror!"

Pitt was reading over William's shoulder. "And that means we have won, my friends," he declared. "Not formally yet. But it is only a matter of time before Parliament outlaws the trade. The Members will eventually give in to the will of the people."

William fell back against the cushion with relief. "I thought I had failed. For a moment I forgot that it was the Lord's work and not mine."

"We are all instruments, William," said Thomas, "me and my stealthy horse, our wily Prime Minister here, and your elegant tongue."

William suddenly remembered a letter from the old sea captain, John Newton. "The wisdom we ask of God is freely given, though we may be said to sometimes pay dearly for it," Newton had written. "Yet it is well worth the purchase, whatever it may cost us."

"We may yet change the world, gentlemen," said William, finally smiling again. "Let's get back to work. We'll have time to sleep later!"

William Wilberforce's speech did not immediately end the slave trade as he had hoped, but it did go down in history as exposing the vile nature of slavery. Despite his ill health, William and the Society for the Abolition of the Slave Trade continued their efforts. On March 25, 1807, a year after the death of William Pitt, Parliament passed the Abolition of the Slave Trade Act.

Making the trade illegal was just the first step of many in changing the way the world thought about slavery. It would be another 25 years, in 1833, before existing slaves were legally freed in Britain. Wilberforce died just three days later.

WILLIAM CAREY:
FRUIT FOR ETERNAL LIFE

NOVEMBER 1800. SERAMPORE, INDIA.

WILLIAM CAREY RAN across the square, his short legs pumping. "*Maaf korben!*" he shouted. "Excuse me!"

The open air market smelled heavily of spices, grilled meat, and animal dung. No one could hear Carey's shouting above the bleating of lambs and customers haggling over sacks of rice, wool, and glass beads. But Carey kept going, parting the crowd as he pushed his way past stall after stall. Dark-haired women in gold and blue saris and men in turbans scattered to get out of the hurried Englishman's way.

On the other side of the market he followed the road past a cluster of huts and down to the wide river the locals called Hoogly. He spotted his friends outside a small house near the riverbank. Dr. John Thomas and Joshua Marshman were leaning over an Indian man writhing in pain on the ground.

"Glad you got the message, William," called Joshua.

"Crocodile attack?" he replied breathlessly.

"No. He just stumbled in the river while he was washing and landed badly. His name is Krishna Pal."

The man was praying through gritted teeth. William recognized the words of a traditional prayer in the local Bengali language.

John straightened up from examining the patient. "He has a dislocated shoulder. We're going to have to reset it."

William wiped the dust and perspiration from his forehead, noticing again that it seemed wider. The Indian climate seemed to be bad for his hairline! He kneeled down and introduced himself to Krishna in Bengali. He told him they were going to fix his arm, but that it was going to be painful at first.

Krishna nodded.

They helped him sit up. William quoted Scripture and talked quietly with him while Joshua ran for a length of rope. Carefully, they tied him against a tree to steady him while Dr. John forced the shoulder back into place. His scream of pain was followed by a loud popping sound, and the arm again rested in its proper place.

Krishna slumped with relief. "*Dhanyabad*," he said.

"You're welcome," Dr. John replied, and repeated it in Bengali. "*Swagatam*."

They helped their new friend into his house and tucked him into the alcove of mosquito netting over his bed. Dr. John gave him some instructions for letting his arm heal properly, and took the opportunity to mention the disease of sin and the healing power of Jesus. Krishna nodded politely. William left a stack of leaflets for the patient to read while he rested.

"I trust one of you will check on him later," William suggested as they walked back to the mission house. "Perhaps you can take him some more reading materials."

"How many years has it been now?" asked Joshua.

William knew what he meant. "Yes, yes. Seven years in India without a convert." He sighed. "A Baptist with no one to baptize."

"Seven years of befriending the people, visiting their homes, preaching, running the school, giving them medical aid, printing the Bible in their language——." Joshua shook his head. "I can understand why you expected to have a whole church of native converts by now."

"It's the caste system," said Dr. John. "The Indian people believe they are meant to remain in whatever social status they are born into. If they throw off caste, they will be rejected by their families and business partners. The people of the higher castes fear the loss of their honor and wealth. The people of the lower castes fear the revenge of their idols. So much is at stake."

"If only they would understand that Christ makes us all equals!"

"The Spirit of God will have to show them that," said William. "Many missionaries have failed to bring change because they insist that the native people become just like them—dressing like them, eating like them, singing like them. We are doing something different. We are bringing the gospel to the people in their language. And when we do have a convert, we will train him to preach and he will lead his people."

Dr. John turned to Joshua. "Before you arrived, the British governor-general in Calcutta once asked William why he didn't just force the Hindus to become Christians. You know what William said in reply? 'The thing is impossible, My Lord. We can force people to be hypocrites, but no power on earth can force them to become Christians!' So we labor waiting for an unearthly power to change their hearts."

William nodded vigorously. "I am so encouraged by our Lord's expression that 'He who works receives wages and gathers fruit for eternal life.' If I am to be like King David, only the instrument for gathering materials, and someone else will build the temple, I hope to find joy in that."

"Well said, sir," agreed Joshua. "That reminds me of the message of an excellent book. In my quiet time I am reading Mr. Jonathan

Edwards' biography of David Brainerd. He, too, learned to trust in God for the success of his mission work."

"I would like to borrow that book when you are finished reading it," said William. "And I am pleased to hear that your Bengali is much improved."

"I cannot give a whole sermon in the language yet."

"Give it time. It has taken me all these years in India and I still falter. Speaking of sermons, in the morning I preach at the great tree in town."

"And in the evening I will be preaching where the four roads meet," said Dr. John.

"Then we both have sermons to prepare," William said as they approached the mission house. "See you at dinner."

The large brick house had a long porch overlooking the River Ganges and several outbuildings. At the courtyard, the men went their separate ways. Each of the missionary families had their own apartment in the house, living and working as a community. It was far from perfect, but it was the beginning of what William had dreamed of when he founded the Baptist Missionary Society several years earlier.

Five families now shared their possessions and their household duties. The men took turns leading prayer and preaching for their Sunday services and on other days throughout the villages. William kept the treasury. Joshua tutored English and Indian children and managed the library. Another colleague, a fresh-faced young printer named William Ward, supervised the printing press housed in one of the outbuildings. The older children worked a large garden. And everyone relied on Joshua's wife, Hannah. She ran a girls' school, kept the household organized and supplied, cared for the youngest missionary children, and—the hardest job of all—watched over William's wife, Dorothy Carey.

Poor Mrs. Carey. Her condition was not part of William's big missionary dream. She had never wanted to leave England and move her children across the ocean. But the thought of the family being separated—maybe forever—was too much to bear. So she finally agreed. But she hated being in India. She had no friends, the food made her sick, and they kept moving from village to village. And then the whole family became terribly ill, and their five-year-old son Peter died. A madness overcame her. She often shouted at people, and sometimes pitched dishes or candlesticks at them. So most days, the community members kept her locked in her room so she couldn't hurt anyone.

What else could they do? William refused to send her away to a cold asylum far from her family. But returning to England was also out of the question. Now that they had a printing press and were translating the Bible into Bengali, he was certain they were finally making progress on the mission field. To leave now would be to give up on the work God had sent them to do. So with Hannah Marshman's guidance, he tried to care for Dorothy as best they could at the mission house.

William let himself into their apartment. He was grateful to find Dorothy sleeping quietly in her room. He went into his small study and sat down at the desk. His Hebrew Bible and a new page of the Bengali translation were sitting where he had left them that morning. Taking up his notebook, he turned his thoughts to tomorrow's sermon, and worked on it until dinnertime.

Early the next morning, William threaded his way through the busy dirt roads. The day was already warm. He could feel the moist breeze coming off the Hoogly River before he reached it. Turning down a lane near the riverbank, he soon found Krishna's house. The patient greeted him with a smile.

"How are you faring today?" William asked.

"The arm is still sore," replied Krishna, "but much better. I am pleased at your visit. Your friends stopped by last night, but I wanted to thank you, too, for helping me yesterday."

"I was glad to help."

Krishna waved to a rug spread under a shady tree and invited his guest to sit. A woman appeared immediately with glasses of cold mint tea. Her ivory and gold bracelets clinked against the glass as she handed it to William. She was wearing a turquoise sari and her bare feet were decorated with painted red designs, a sign that she was married.

"Dr. Carey, I present my wife, Rasamayi."

"*Nomoskar*," said William. "Hello."

She lowered her dark eyes politely and gave him a half-smile.

Another person was hovering in the curtained doorway. Krishna waved the young man to join them on the rug. "This is my friend Gokul," he said to his guest.

Gokul reached to shake William's hand in the European fashion. "Hello, Dr. Carey."

"*Nomoskar*, Gokul," William said. "I saw you here yesterday, I believe."

"Yes. I was the one who went to see if Dr. John could help Krishna."

"Ah." William turned to Krishna. "It is good to see you healing, and very nice to meet your family and friends." He took a drink of the refreshing tea and then returned to the purpose of his visit. "I would like to invite you to come to our mission house. Dr. John can give you something for the pain until you are fully healed."

"That is kind of you. But," said Krishna, his eyes darting up the road, "it is best if I am not seen there."

"We do not practice the caste," William said firmly. "The Christian gospel is one of equality. Men and women, slaves and free peoples, rich and poor. All are equals in Jesus. There is no reason to be ashamed for visiting an English house."

Krishna shook his head. "It is not so simple for Hindus. But I will consider your offer."

"I hope you will. Dr. John and Brother Marshman said you read the pamphlets we gave you."

Every time the missionaries visited someone's home, they brought gospel tracts they had printed in Bengali on their own press. Each one contained a verse of Scripture and a short message. One they had left for Krishna read: "He who confesses and forsakes his sins, and trusts in the righteousness of Christ, obtains salvation."

"Yes, I read the materials," nodded Krishna. "The ideas are strange but interesting."

"What do you find most strange?"

"Your idea of sin," said Krishna, setting down his glass so he could gesture with his hands. "We Hindus believe that we sin against ourselves only. We believe in karma—what we do in this life affects our next life. If we are a good person in this life, we come back as a good person the next time. But if we are evil, we come back in a lesser form, as a member of a lower caste or perhaps even an animal. That is just how it is. So there is no need to confess sin or seek salvation."

"I see. But, Krishna, the Christian Bible teaches something different. We believe that sin is an offense against a holy God. A person who offends God—and everyone does—is in danger of eternal punishment."

"You mean 'Hell.' I read about that place in your pamphlets."

"It is the place of judgment for those who reject God's way of salvation through his son Jesus."

"So says your Bible. But that is not written in our *Shastras*."

"I am going to preach about your *Shastras* today, under the great tree. Will you come listen?" He looked expectantly at both men.

Krishna and Gokul glanced at each other. "Perhaps we may."

"Well, thank you for the conversation," said William, getting to his feet. He noticed movement at the door of the house as the curtain fluttered into place. "And please thank your wife for the delicious tea," he added.

An hour later, he was standing on a flat rock in the shelter of a massive banyan tree. The thick branches sent off so many roots into the ground that the one tree appeared to have dozens of trunks. It had grown there for as long as the villagers could remember, and for years they had held their town meetings in the coolness of its leafy canopy. To William, it was the perfect place for open air preaching.

"I have been reading your *Shastras*," he was saying now. "Their language is very beautiful. But they all say different things. Some of you follow one *Shastra*, and some of you follow another. How do you know which ones are true?"

He looked out on the few dozen people gathered around him. The crowd was constantly shifting, as groups of workers on their way to and from the village paused out of curiosity. He recognized a few men who came and sat there every day. They seemed to listen carefully, but never stayed to talk afterward. And not everyone was there to hear him preach. An old woman and her skinny dog were taking advantage of the shade, dozing as flies buzzed around their heads.

"Your *Shastras*," he continued, "are like loaves of bread baked with a bit of poison. They contain good and healthy things but also bits of false teachings. And those false teachings make the rest of the bread bad. That is how the Christian Bible is different, my friends. The gospel of Christ is pure, through and through. It contains all knowledge for salvation and joyful living. Read it, and you will see the difference."

As he always did, he concluded his sermon by passing out the Scripture pamphlets he translated and Brother Ward printed. Most people politely took the pamphlets, but he had no idea how many actually read them.

The crowd dispersed, except for the old lady who was still sleeping. But as he turned to go, he was surprised to find Krishna and Gokul waiting to speak to him.

"We kept talking after you left," said Gokul, "and we decided to come listen."

"And we have some questions," added Krishna. "May we walk with you back to your house?"

"Of course! Of course!" And he gladly answered their questions as they made their way back through the village.

Krishna and Gokul began to meet with the missionaries every day. They went to hear them preach, studied their pamphlets, and sat with them in the evenings asking questions.

One night, William and Joshua went to see Krishna after dinner. Gokul joined them. As usual, they sat on the rug outside and drank Rasamayi's mint tea. But instead of hiding in the doorway, Rasamayi now sat nearby listening. She had even invited her sister Jaymani. The two women pretended to concentrate on their needlework, in case the neighbors were watching, but their ears were tuned to the missionaries.

"Krishna," said William, "we cannot tell you how excited we are that your family is interested in the Christian gospel."

"We are also excited to know more. But I have sorrow for my friend." He looked at Gokul.

Gokul's eyes were lowered in shame. "It is my wife, Dr. Carey," he said. "I told her of my interest in following Christ. She became angry and said I had disgraced her. She and my mother have left my house and refuse to return."

"Where are they now?"

"My wife has returned to her father, and my mother has gone to my brother's house."

"Perhaps they would come with you to our Bengali worship meeting?" suggested Joshua.

Gokul shook his head. "We have argued for many hours. They do not believe that the Bible is the word of God. I told them, as you told us, that it is pure in its commands and that its contents are without flaw. But they do not believe me. They believe the old ways, and according to the old ways, I am to be shunned for bringing shame on them."

"I'm so sorry," said William. "I can only pray that your family will come to see the truth and return to you. Jesus spoke a hard truth when he taught that we must be willing to leave father and mother to follow him, if that is necessary."

"But, my brother, you shall not be alone," Krishna said with a welcoming smile. "We will be your family. Together we believe, and together we shall endure."

Without looking up from their needlework, the two women murmured their agreement.

"Please, brothers, come to the mission house tomorrow for the midday meal," said William suddenly.

Krishna and Gokul glanced at each other hesitantly. "If we eat with you in public—."

"Yes," said Joshua. "You will have broken with the caste if you eat with us. But if you are to come to Christ, you must do as he did and treat all of his people as equal before God."

"We will consider it," said Krishna finally.

At noon the next day, a table was set on the porch of the mission house. Dorothy Carey was feeling ill, but the rest of the missionaries had pitched in to prepare for visitors. Hannah Marshman had spent all morning in the kitchen with the two orphaned Indian girls who worked for her. "Curry and rice on plantain leaves," William had asked her to serve. "Our first meal in India and still my favorite."

The covered dishes were set out on the table. The cold tea was poured. The missionaries gathered on the porch. But their guests had not arrived.

How many times had they invited the locals to dinner and were disappointed? William was sure he could hear the servants muttering that they had cooked too much food and that no Hindu would come to a Christian table. He began to feel despair.

But then as he stared down the road, the shapes of two men appeared in the glare of the sun, and Krishna and Gokul stepped into the courtyard of the mission house.

"The Spirit of God does move indeed!" declared Joshua.

William restrained himself from throwing his arms around their guests. "Come enjoy our table!" he cried. He said a long prayer of gratitude and then the girls scurried to dish up the food.

The missionaries had chosen a public place to set their table. As they ate, villagers coming down the road cast shocked glances at the two Hindu men eating with the English Christians. Krishna and Gokul stayed put, but they were clearly nervous, knowing the gossip would be all over town before they finished their meal.

Later, Krishna and Rasamayi, her sister Jaymani, and Gokul all came to the mission house to join the missionaries for their evening worship. John Thomas opened the service with prayer, and then the four Indians took turns telling about the change Jesus was bringing to their souls. William was overjoyed.

He was working in his study the following afternoon, writing a letter to the Baptist Missionary Society back home, when he heard shouting from the road. Grabbing his hat, he ran out to the courtyard. Gokul stood there panting, telling Joshua between deep gulps of air that Krishna's family had been arrested.

"Arrested! What happened?" William demanded.

"Years ago, Krishna and Rasamayi agreed to give their daughter to a man in Calcutta when she was old enough to marry. But now that they are following Christ, they have backed out of their agreement. They do not want her to marry a Hindu. The bridegroom is very angry and has come from Calcutta to take her anyway. A mob of his relatives broke into Krishna's house and dragged them all away!"

Joshua could not believe it. "The neighbors did not stop the mob?"

"The neighbors cheered for them!" Gokul said, eyes flashing. "They want the governor to order Krishna to give his daughter as he promised. They don't want their neighbors and relatives to start going back on their agreements."

"I know the governor," said William. "Colonel Bie is a good

man. I'm sure he will help us."

Joshua shook his head. "It's his job to keep the peace. If he lets Krishna go, the people might become violent."

"Then you and I must go now and speak to him," insisted William, heading toward the road. He called to Gokul over his shoulder. "Go to the printing press and tell Brother Ward where we are!"

The two missionaries hurried to the house of Colonel Bie, the Danish governor of the Serampore colony. But he wasn't home. So they hurried on to the prison to make sure Krishna and his family had not been harmed.

As soon as they reached the brick administration office at the prison, they saw Krishna coming out of the building with his family. "Dr. Carey!" he cried.

"I am so glad to see you are unharmed," said William. "Tell me what has happened."

"The governor released us."

"He did? Why?" insisted Joshua.

"Because I can't see they have done any wrong," said a voice behind them.

William turned to see the governor standing in the doorway, his hand outstretched. "Dr. Carey. Mr. Marshman. It is good to see you both again."

William took the Dane's hand in a firm grip. "We are glad to see you, Colonel. We were on our way to your office to plead the case of our friends here."

"No need, Carey. No law recognized by Denmark has been broken, and I do not believe that this man can be required to give his daughter to anyone. If the groom wants to file a grievance, he should do it through the British government in Calcutta. I don't know about you Brits, but I don't tolerate angry mobs in my colony!"

"In that case," said William, drawing the governor out of earshot of the others, "would you be willing to go a step further? Krishna is the first Hindu in our town to voluntarily reject the caste. Folks around here are angry. I am worried that the neighbors who cheered his attack this morning might try to do him more harm while he sleeps."

"You suspect a murder attempt?"

"Don't you think it's possible? We are to baptize them on the next Lord's Day. If you could provide some protection for them until then, I would feel much better."

"They are converts then? This is an accomplishment for your mission, Carey. I congratulate you. Well, I will post guards tonight and ensure their safety, as far as my power and rights allow."

"Thank you, Colonel. Perhaps you would also care to attend the baptism on Sunday?"

"I would be delighted. In fact, I have some diplomatic guests in town and I would like them to see what you're doing down on the river. By the way, how is Mrs. Carey?"

William's face clouded. "I'm afraid her condition is the same."

"Poor thing." Colonel Bie gave him a sympathetic look.

After another round of thank-yous, William herded them out of the gate and made sure Krishna's family arrived home securely. The presence of the governor's guards seemed to get the attention of the neighborhood, and the mob did not reappear.

William and Joshua spent the rest of the week at their best preaching spots, explaining why Krishna and his family had left the Hindu religion. Word about their rejection of caste and the mob attack had spread throughout the region, making people more curious about the message of the missionaries. Some listened intently, even with sympathy. But others mocked them and called Krishna a heretic.

On Sunday afternoon, a small crowd spread rugs on the banks of the River Ganges in front of the mission house. It was December 28, 1800, a long seven years after William had arrived in India.

Krishna, Rasamayi, Gokul, and Jaymani were to be baptized today. He was feeling double joy, because today he would also be baptizing his son Felix, who had recently declared himself a Christian. His only regret was that Dorothy was in bed with another fever and couldn't join them outside.

True to his promise, Colonel Bie came for the service. With him were some of the local high-ranking Hindu officials, Muslim leaders, and visiting dignitaries from Europe. They made a colorful mix of jeweled turbans, black robes, and lace-throated waistcoats as they joined the missionary families under the trees.

Standing before the wide stretch of water, Brother Ward opened the service with a sermon, in English, on John 5:39. He called the hearers to "search the Scriptures." Then William stood and preached in Bengali about the meaning of baptism. Rivers are sacred in the Hindu religion, so he took care to remind everyone that they were to put off all idols, including the gods of the river, and embrace Christ alone.

When he finished, he turned toward the gate near the water's edge, and motioned for the converts to come down. There was some shuffling in the grass, but the gate stayed closed.

He caught Felix's eye and gestured for him to come. Felix nodded and nudged the others. But when they swung the gate open, only Felix and Krishna came down to the water.

"They are afraid," Krishna whispered to the missionary.

William was stunned. "Now? After all they have already been through?" he thought. Well, there would be time to talk later and calm their fears, he decided. This moment was for Felix and Krishna.

In the midday heat, the surface of the water shimmered like gold. He led the two men down into the river. The cool liquid rushed past his ankles, then his knees, and then submerged him to his waist. Standing there in the water with his son and his new son in the faith was like a refreshing bath for his soul.

He baptized Felix first. "In the name of the Father, Son, and Holy Spirit," he declared. He couldn't help embracing the boy as he emerged from the water.

Then Krishna came to stand beside him. "Krishna Pal has asked to tell us why he is being baptized today," William said, looking especially at the Hindu leaders sitting on the bank. "Go ahead, brother," he urged Krishna.

Krishna cleared his throat. "There is no happiness outside of Christ," he said, raising his voice so it rang out across the water. "I tried the Hindu worship to no avail. After I heard of Christ, one who was willing to lay down his life for my sin, I thought, what love is this! For this, I am willing to give up all. Here I make my resting place."

When Krishna came up out of the river, he was smiling broadly, shining drops of water running down his brown head.

William followed him to shore, but hesitated in the shallows. On top of a hill downriver, he could just make out the temple of one of the local gods. "Do you tremble today, you false god of stone and clay?" he said under his breath. "Do you fear the sight of your people washing your dust off their feet?"

He looked up on the bank, where the missionaries were embracing the baptized converts. "The first of the Hindus to trample the caste for Christ's sake," he said with satisfaction. "And he will bring a whole continent behind him!"

<hr />

William Carey founded the Baptist Missionary Society in 1792. He has been called the "father of modern missions" because he used methods friendly to the cultures of those he evangelized. He is also called the "father of Bengali prose," due to the number of books he translated into that language and his later work as a professor of Bengali at Fort William College. He translated the Bible into many different Indian languages. Like William Wilberforce and Elizabeth Fry, he believed Christians should lead the way in social reform. He urged the Indian governments to outlaw the practice of infanticide (leaving babies to die) and sati (the burning of a widow with her husband's body at his death). He also founded a horticultural society. He was greatly assisted by his colleagues, Joshua Marshman (1768-1837) andWilliamWard (1769-1823).

Dorothy never recovered from her many illnesses and died unhappy in 1807.William remarried Charlotte Rumohr until her death in 1821, and later married Grace Hughes. He died on June 9, 1834.

Krishna Pal's family and friends were baptized soon after him. He invited neighbors into his home to learn about Christ and started a preaching school for Indian converts.With the testimony and assistance of Krishna Pal, over 1,400 new converts were added by 1821.

ELIZABETH FRY: LAUDABLE PURSUITS

JANUARY 1813. NEWGATE STREET, LONDON.

THREE WOMEN STEPPED onto the scaffold. Their bare feet, chained together, shuffled across the wooden planks, lodging splinters in their heels. Faces dirty and clothing in rags, they didn't even look at the row of nooses hanging before them.

For the prisoners, it was their day to die. For the onlookers, it was a typical Monday morning. A crowd gathered in the prison courtyard to watch the hanging, from rich merchants with fat wallets to pickpockets waiting to relieve them of those burdens. Even the governor, from his apartment above the square, sat back and watched while he lingered over the last bites of his breakfast.

One by one, the executioner draped the ropes around the prisoners' necks and gently pulled them snug. Each of the women looked down to see their swollen feet framed by a door—their entrance into the next life. With the chiming of the death knell, the doors below them opened and they fell into eternity.

In the crowd was a man with dark eyebrows that stood out from his neatly-cropped white hair. Stephen Grellet did not watch the execution, but instead observed the mixed reactions in the crowd. Only an hour before he had talked to some of the prisoners on their way to the gallows. Some were murderers or kidnappers. But many of them were guilty of lesser crimes, like cutting down trees, passing fake money—or one of the other two hundred offenses punishable by death.

He turned his serious face on the man next to him. "We can't forget what we've seen here today, William."

William Forster gave him a grim nod. "That man we met earlier, the one being executed tomorrow, told me that despite his dire situation, he considered Jesus his refuge and strength."

"If only all the prisoners could hear the gospel," said Stephen. "In these English jails, execution is handed out more freely than water. Some of them haven't even had a trial or been convicted! No human being should have to live in these conditions."

"Is there nothing we can do?"

Stephen considered this as they moved toward the gate. His sorrow and frustration must have been obvious, because a guard sniffed at them as they passed. "Do not cry for them, Frenchman. They are the dogs of our city."

Anger swelled in Stephen's chest as he turned on the guard. "No, your dogs get scraps from your table! But to your needy fellow Englishmen you give nothing."

William pulled him out onto the street. After the close confines of the crowded courtyard, the cold wet air in the street was refreshing. Stephen took a deep breath and let the city traffic pass by him. Clopping horses and squealing carriage wheels splashed through puddles and left streaking trails of mud across the brick street. A boy hawked newspapers. A toothless man begged for food. Ladies held the elbows of gentlemen, ignoring the mud clinging to the hems of their dresses.

"They're oblivious," Stephen thought. They walked a few paces down the street, and then he turned back with a final look at the prison. It was a dark stone building, the roof and few windows outlined with white trim. Smokestacks poured black smoke into the gray sky. The smell lingered in his throat. "That prison is cold and black," he thought, "like London's heart."

A carriage halted on the street in front of them. The driver jumped down and opened the door. "Monsieur Grellet, shall we go?"

Stephen and William climbed in.

"To Mildred's Court, please," said Stephen. "We must talk to Elizabeth."

"Yes, Monsieur," said the driver through the window.

At Mildred's Court, Elizabeth Fry was in the apartment she shared with her husband on the second floor of the Fry family's tea import business. They had a house in the country, but often stayed in the London apartment for weeks at a time when business was heavy. She missed her children when she was away, so visits from her friends were bright spots in her work.

Today she was joined by her brother, Joseph Gurney, and their friend, Anna Buxton. Elizabeth and Anna were dressed as Quakers, in plain white dresses, white bonnets, and brown shawls. Elizabeth's family was still unhappy about her decision to become a Plain Quaker, since the Quakers were known as dissenters. But her brother, Joseph, kept in close contact with her. And today, he and Anna were enjoying a good-natured argument over the teachings of the Quakers. Elizabeth sat nearby, happy to share their company while she re-read *The Pilgrim's Progress*.

She found herself staring out the window as the carriage of a rich neighbor passed the house. What fine horses they were driving! She loved extravagant things, and her husband could afford them, but she denied herself. She was determined to live in the plain style of the Quakers. She prayed every day to stay true to her convictions, but it was not easy, especially when she compared herself to her neighbors.

"Betsy!" Anna shouted suddenly. "Tell your brother I'm right."

Elizabeth turned back to them. "I'm sorry. I must have been daydreaming. What are you right about this time?"

But the sitting room door opened and Stephen and William came in. Their faces were gray.

Elizabeth crossed quickly to welcome them. "My dears, are you alright?"

Anna drew up two more chairs, forgetting about her argument.

"I've seen many things in my life," said Stephen, shaking his head. "But I have never seen the evils of man like I have today."

Elizabeth poured glasses of water and handed them around. "What happened?"

Stephen shot a grim look at William. "We have been on a private tour of Newgate Prison. We had to see for ourselves if things are as bad there as we have heard."

"And?" prompted Anna.

"We saw both the men's and women's sections," William said. "I've never seen such terrible living conditions! Men, women, children, even infants—all of them—living like animals."

Stephen turned to his hostess. "Have you ever seen anything like that before, Betsy?"

Elizabeth sat back in her chair and sighed. "We often ministered to the poor when I was a child, and before we married I tutored some children in great need, but I have never been to Newgate before. I've only heard of the atrocities that happen there."

"I hear people are sometimes hanged without a trial," suggested Joseph.

Stephen nodded.

"And the hangings have become a spectacle," added Anna with disgust. "People watch the executions for entertainment."

"Punishment is not about having revenge," said Elizabeth.

"Punishment is to remind criminals that there are penalties for crime, so as to lessen the number of crimes and to hopefully bring redemption to the criminal."

"As Jesus would have it," said Stephen. "Unfortunately, the citizens of London have forgotten about redemption."

"Is there something the Quaker Friends can do about it?" asked Elizabeth.

"I think you should visit the prison," said Stephen. "See for yourself."

"And take them some basic supplies," suggested William. "They could use clothing and blankets."

Elizabeth sat up taller in her chair. "That is a wonderful idea. I have some free time since the children are back in Plashet, and I've been thinking of specific ways we could use our wealth for the Lord. Perhaps this is my opportunity."

"I will help you," Anna said. "We will call our friends together and ask them to donate clothes, then deliver them to the prison."

"It is a good thing. But be warned, sisters," Stephen said with a grim face, "the prison is a very disturbing place. The inmates desperately need the light of Christ."

"Then we will shine that light in the darkest corner of London!" Elizabeth cried.

Elizabeth and Anna began to collect clothes for their trip to Newgate. Some of their friends thought they were crazy for wanting to go to the prison at all. But other friends were glad to donate old and new clothes to pass out to the women inmates.

They also had to get permission from the governor to enter the prison. At first, he was not comfortable with the idea of letting the two women in. He himself refused to visit the women's section of the prison. But Elizabeth was well-known in the community and insisted on helping the prisoners. So he finally gave them a permit to visit.

The morning of their tour, Elizabeth and Anna unloaded bags of clothing from their carriage at the entrance. The guard inspected their permit and shook his head. "You're a crazy lot for wanting to go in there," he declared. "Enter at your own risk. The guards ain't obligated to protect you."

Behind the gate a shouting arose as a group of prisoners were transported. Elizabeth and Anna glanced at each other nervously but set their shoulders. When the guard opened the gate, they dragged their bags with them.

They stopped first at the warden's office. The warden shook his head at their permit, too. "I don't know why you want to do this, but since you have the governor's permission, I won't stop you. But you really should leave your belongings here. The animals inside will take everything you have."

"We've brought these bags of clothes for the women," Elizabeth insisted. "We have to take them in."

"At least leave your watch here," said the warden, eyeing the gold circle in Elizabeth's pocket.

The watch was an engagement gift from her husband, so she decided to leave it in the warden's care. But she was determined to carry everything else in with her.

He instructed the guards to unbolt the massive doors and then secure them again behind the women. They stepped in, and the iron bolts rang as they were rammed back into place.

Elizabeth and Anna were inside Newgate Prison.

A sickening odor filled the hall at the entrance of the women's section of the prison. They found themselves in front of two large cells, dark and filthy. Behind the bars were three or four hundred people. Young girls, old women, and mothers holding infants huddled together. Most were barely clothed. A few were trying to wash their clothes in pots of putrid water.

A blur of rags and hair in the corner immediately got their attention. Two women rolled on the ground, clawing at each other. Elizabeth pulled Anna back as the guards stepped in and knocked the two tumbling women apart with threats of beating.

When they saw Elizabeth and Anna, a hush fell over the cells. Then suddenly the women and children rushed forward, begging for food and clothing. Their shrieks made the two friends step back in alarm again.

"Betsy," cried Anna, "what do we do now?"

"We have to do what we came here to do," said Elizabeth, steeling herself for the task. She reached in her bag and started handing dresses and shawls through the bars. She tried to give the clothes to those who needed them most, but the women snatched them away from each other.

"Is this all you have?" demanded one woman, ripping a shawl from the girl Elizabeth had given it to.

But some of the women had tears in their eyes. "Bless you, my lady," one woman whispered. "Yes, thank you, kind lady," called a girl behind her.

As the prisoners greedily wrapped themselves in the new clothes and cried out blessings to Elizabeth, she realized the influence she could have. "O Lord," she prayed, "preserve me from the temptation to think of myself as better than these women. Keep me humble and show me how I can serve them."

At Anna's gasp, Elizabeth turned to look where her friend was pointing. In the corner, two women knelt over a dead baby. They were stripping off his clothes to put on another crying infant.

Elizabeth ran toward them, pulling a bundle of flannel baby clothes out of her bag. "Please!" she cried. "Take these."

The two women froze and stared at her. She looked into their hollow eyes, where tears were forming streaks of filth down their cheeks.

"Take these," she urged again. "Your babies should have fresh clothes."

"Our babies shouldn't be in here!" spat one of the women.

She glanced at the dead baby and held back the sickening feeling in her stomach. "I know," she said tenderly. "I have children, too."

"I shouldn't be here either!" the woman shouted. "I ain't done nothin' wrong but try to feed my babies."

Elizabeth didn't know what else to say to her. She stared down at the moldy straw on the floor, then straightened up suddenly. "Listen, everyone! Ladies, please," she called in her firm voice. "In our bags we have plenty of flannel clothes for infants. They will keep your babies warm. Please, those of you who have little ones in here, step forward."

The crowd glared at her with suspicion.

She held a fistful of flannel above her head. "If we run out, we'll bring more."

The hardened faces softened, and women began to step aside so the mothers could come to the front. Elizabeth and Anna emptied their bags into the women's hands. Soon dozens of babies had been clothed in new flannel garments. The mothers gazed on the visitors with grateful eyes.

"We'll return next week with more clothes for the rest of you," Elizabeth promised them. "Maybe we can bring some other necessities, too."

When the guards let them back out onto the street, Elizabeth and Anna gulped in the sour city air like it was a fresh meadow breeze. They barely spoke, each unable to forget the images of the wayward women now forced to live like mistreated cattle.

That night, Elizabeth sat in her tin bathtub long after the water turned cold. As hard as she scrubbed, she could not wash away the smell of those girls rotting in prison.

Elizabeth and Anna wasted no time collecting more supplies for the prisoners. Elizabeth went to the Quaker Meeting as she did every Sunday and afterwards convinced the other women to donate shoes and shawls and dresses. They purchased medicines and bandages. They even collected several copies of the Bible, though most of the women in the prison didn't know how to read.

Within a few days they had big baskets full of supplies to deliver to the prisoners. The warden shook his head in disbelief again. The heavy doors clanged shut again. And Elizabeth and Anna were again standing in the dark, foul-smelling cells of the women's section of the prison.

As their eyes adjusted to the darkness, they saw that some of the girls and their babies were still wearing their new clothes. But others had traded them to the guards for alcohol and were dancing wildly. Elizabeth realized that the prisoners had more problems than just being poor and locked away. In their cages, they had given up all civilized behavior.

"These women need food, moral discipline, and education," she said to Anna.

Anna looked at her thoughtfully. "We know a lot of high-ranking people. Maybe we can use our influence to do more than just deliver supplies."

"Yes! We can do so much good for these women!" Elizabeth nodded eagerly. But as she passed out the clothes and Bibles, the prisoners praised her and thanked her. A familiar, uneasy feeling spread through her body.

That night, Elizabeth could not sleep. She wanted to help the suffering prisoners, but something was bothering her. She wasn't sure what it was until she lit the oil lamp by her bed and began to write in her journal.

The last few days I've feared for myself. I'm afraid that my good state in life, the support of my friends for my work, and being engaged in laudable pursuits—especially my work among the prisoners—will tempt me to be prideful. Oh, how deeply I fear the temptation of being conceited! Be pleased, O Lord, to preserve me. The deep prayer of my heart is to walk humbly before you and also before all human beings. Let me never take the glory that belongs to you. In your mercy, let your unworthy servant do good.

It wasn't the first time she had written such a prayer in her journal. She came from a rich family and grew up with fine dresses and silver dishes. Ever since she had become a Quaker, she had tried to live in their simple style and treat all people equally. But it was hard to do. She knew only the Lord could help her keep a humble attitude.

The next day Anna arrived at her door with a carriage full of baskets. "Are you ready to go back to the prison today?" Anna called to her. "Last night, I picked up several items from friends that will help the older women at Newgate. Also, I have some men's clothes we could give to the warden for the male prisoners."

"Of course," said Elizabeth.

They arrived at Newgate again. As they passed by, the guards mumbled to each other about the crazy women who thought they could make wild prisoners into good people.

This time, while Anna passed out her supplies, Elizabeth climbed up on a wooden crate and began to preach to the women. She told them the clothes and other gifts were from Christians who wanted to bless them with the love of Christ. She told them only Christ could deliver them from their eternal prison.

"Even if your bodies are doomed to Newgate, your souls can be free if you trust in Jesus," rang her message through the cells.

Soon some of the women began to move closer and sit where they could hear her better. Elizabeth could see tears in the eyes of some of the girls. Even those who had been dancing quieted and drew near. Soon they were all listening to her message.

She was thrilled that the prisoners wanted to hear about Jesus. But in her heart, she again felt the evil she had written about in her journal. She noticed how their eyes admired her pretty features and clean clothes, how they were impressed by her proper speech and comforting voice. Oh, how she loved the attention! Her pride swelled up like a twisted creature in her breast.

The following week when Anna knocked on Elizabeth's door, she was surprised to find her friend in the middle of packing.

"Aren't you ready to go to the Newgate with me?" she said, navigating around the cases and trunks on the sitting room floor.

"I can't go," said Elizabeth gravely. "It is bad for my spirit."

"How can helping others be bad for your spirit?" asked Anna, furling her eyebrows in confusion.

Elizabeth looked at the floor. "It brings me pride to do something for them. I feel as if I'm the center of attention, the star."

"That's because you are! You're the one with the ability to help them, and they are desperate for that help."

"But I'm a Quaker," reminded Elizabeth. "We don't believe we should be above anyone. That is why we don't call men Mister or Sir. That is why we wear plain clothing. That is why we call this place Mildred's Court and not Saint Mildred's Court. Only Christ deserves praise. If I do this, I will find myself sinning."

Anna was quiet for a moment. "Very well, Betsy. I believe this work is worthy of your attention, but if you cannot do it in good conscience, you cannot do it."

Elizabeth nodded. "I'm packing my things because I am heading back to Plashet in a few days. With all my business in the city, I haven't seen my husband or my children in a while. I've spent more time with the prisoners than with them."

"I understand," Anna said quietly. "Will you continue to help the women of Newgate?"

"In whatever way I can," assured Elizabeth.

Traveling back to Plashet, Elizabeth prayed that the time away from the prisoners would cure her from her prideful condition.

But the next few years were dark ones for Elizabeth. She gave birth to another son. She loved being with her children, and she told them about her visits to the prison to warn them about the price of ungodly behavior. But the winters in Plashet were cold and gloomy. She worried about her sins. She ate less and less. She missed serving the prisoners and started a school in her home for poor girls with the help of her neighbor, the vicar's wife. But her joy was soon darkened by the death of her older brother, John, who like most of her family had not approved of her joining the Quakers. Only a few months later, her seventh child, Little Betsy, caught a severe fever and died.

She told her sorrows to her journal: *It pleased the Almighty and Infinite Wisdom to take from us our most dear and beloved child, little Betsy. My loss is almost inexpressible! To wake and find my tenderly beloved little girl so gone from my view! So many pleasant times are now marred.*

Times were hard for London businesses, too. Like other merchants, the Fry family business was losing money. Elizabeth and her family were forced to give up the house in Plashet and move back to Mildred's Court. There, Elizabeth gave birth to another boy. She was soon distressed by her older daughters who didn't want to be Plain Quakers like their parents.

By Christmas 1816, Elizabeth feared she was facing another depressing winter. She sat watching snowflakes drift past the window. Impulsively, she picked up her journal. Flipping through the pages, she spotted an entry from four years earlier. Days before Stephen Grellet had arrived to tell her about Newgate Prison, she had written: "I fear that my life is slipping away to little purpose."

"But I did find purpose then," she said to herself. "I brought the hope of the gospel and the help of a sister to the women prisoners."

In the years since then, she had felt something was missing. And now she realized what it was. "God gave me moral sensibilities and the gift of leadership. He called me to serve the women society had forgotten, and I rejected them because I was afraid. Instead of fighting my prideful desires, I simply ran away from them!"

She knew what she had to do now, for her own soul and the souls of the poor women. It was time to return to her ministry at Newgate.

She began to make regular visits again. She preached to them about the pains of hell and the glories of heaven. She reminded them that they could respect each other even if society didn't respect them, that they could treat each other with kindness. She encouraged the women to teach their children to sing hymns instead of curse.

And then she had another idea.

"What do you think?" she asked the women gathered around her. "Don't you want a school for your children? Or are these poor babes doomed to grow up as criminals?"

"No one has ever asked us what we think!" was their response. They begged her to help them get a school for their children.

Elizabeth made an appointment to meet with the governor and the warden.

"Your suggestion is admirable, Mrs. Fry," the governor said. "But it simply won't work."

"Why not?"

"These prisoners are wicked and vicious!" the warden interrupted. "They will make a mockery of your school, stealing the books to trade for playing cards and alcohol. It will be a waste of your time."

"If that happens, I will give more books and more time. But I do not think it will happen. I have talked to these women. I have helped them clothe their babies. They want what all mothers want for their children. All I need is your permission to try my experiment."

"But who would teach them? No schoolteacher will take a classroom in a prison."

"Ah, I already have a teacher," Elizabeth announced triumphantly. "One of the prisoners is a young lady named Mary O'Connor. She was a teacher before she was imprisoned for stealing a watch, and she has a tender heart for the little ones. She has already agreed to assist me."

The governor scratched the back of his neck and looked at the warden.

The warden turned to Elizabeth with hands spread. "Of course we wish we could support your effort. But there is just not enough room in the prison for a school. We can't be setting up tables every day, and there isn't one extra cell that could be reserved for school use."

Elizabeth leaned forward in her seat. "So your only objection, then, is one of space?"

"Of course," the governor nodded vigorously.

"I see," she said, rising. "Then I thank you for your time."

Surprised, they stumbled to see her out.

She went immediately back to the women's section of the prison. "How can we come up with the space, sisters?" she asked the disappointed prisoners.

The women looked around their small, damp quarters.

"What if we give up that cell?" replied one woman, pointing. "If we were all willing to share this one, maybe we could have school in that one."

Elizabeth beamed at them. She knew the experiment would work if the women were willing to sacrifice for it. She marched right back to the warden's office, where the governor was still meeting with him.

"The prisoners are willing to move into one cell so the other can be set up as a schoolroom," she announced before they could stand. "Since we now have the space you require, I assume you will grant permission for me to proceed."

The two men stared at each other. Finally, the governor shrugged. "You are a hard person to say no to, Mrs. Fry. Go ahead and try your experiment."

School began the very next day. Elizabeth brought some of her friends to assist the young teacher. The children gathered with wide eyes, eager to learn to how to count and write their names. Soon the women begged Elizabeth to teach them to read and sew so they could earn wages from their cell.

Elizabeth tried to get businessmen to help her set up a sewing business for her women, but the men were convinced the prisoners would steal the cloth. So she called on the vicar's wife in Plashet, who agreed to help. And Anna jumped at the chance to work with Elizabeth again. Soon they had formed the Association for the Improvement of the Female Prisoners of Newgate. The Association members made sure one of them visited the prisoners every day. They taught them to sew and convinced Londoners to buy their products. They raised money to hire a matron to look over their section of the prison.

Soon Elizabeth decided the women prisoners would be safer and better cared for if they had a woman warden and women guards. But how could she convince the authorities?

Her husband suggested she invite them all to Mildred's Court. "The governor, the warden, the sheriff, and the prison minister," he said. "If they all gather around our table and hear you describe the amazing things you have done with those women, I'm sure we can convince them to try your idea."

It was a good plan. After the governor heard what Mr. and Mrs. Fry had to say, he agreed to visit the women's section of the prison the following Sunday and see things for himself.

And he was shocked at what he saw! When he arrived with Elizabeth, the prisoners sat quietly around the walls of their swept cell with repaired clothing and washed faces. Even the children were ready to sit and listen.

Elizabeth stood in the center and began to speak. "My sisters, when I first met you, you knew this prison was a place of torment. And after we spent time together, you learned that there is another place of torment, where the sins of this world are paid for eternally. But you also learned that there is one who paid for our crimes and who can set the prisoner with faith free from that eternal cell."

"Jesus!" the women murmured.

"Yes," said Elizabeth. "And I, too, have learned that only my faith in Christ and my obedience to his call can set me free from my sins. So we have taught each other much. Today I ask you, before the governor, if you will agree to abide by a new prison system. Will you submit yourselves to a woman warden? Will you continue to respect the school here for your children? Will you engage in useful work and commit yourself to Christian kindness and cleanliness and order?"

The prisoners nodded soberly. "We will!"

Elizabeth looked at the governor.

He stepped forward. "Mrs. Fry, I don't know what to say. I never expected to find such hard work and good manners in this prison."

"The praise belongs to God for changing hearts," she replied.

He frowned at the prisoners. "I warn all of you that if you do not strictly obey the rules but begin to display bad behavior, I will order a return to the previous system! But as Mrs. Fry pledges to see this through, I am willing to try her ideas."

Turning, he paused before the members of Elizabeth's Association, who were lined up at the entrance. "This is your project, ladies. I will be keeping an eye on you."

They grinned and nodded as he marched out.

And with that, Elizabeth Fry and her friends had begun a great movement that would bring fair treatment—and the message of the gospel—to prisoners in London and around the world.

Though Elizabeth's brother Joseph Gurney never fully agreed with her Quaker views, he joined her efforts to reform England's prison system. Together they traveled the country to record the injustices in English prisons, challenging the government to make changes. Elizabeth also argued for the fair treatment of the mentally ill, the abolition of slavery, and the improvement of British hospitals. Other Christians implemented her ideas in various countries, including Russia. Elizabeth Gurney Fry died on October 12, 1845.

REV⊕LUTI⊕NS AND REBELLI⊕NS

DURING THE YEARS of the Great Awakenings, several major conflicts redefined the world: the American Revolution, the French Revolution, and the Taiping Rebellion.

THE AMERICAN REVOLUTION

The *American Revolution* was a war for independence by the thirteen British colonies in North America. Many causes led to the war. With Britain thousands of miles away, the colonies made their own governments and mostly managed their own affairs. After the British victory in the French and Indian War (1754-1763), Britain was in financial debt. Parliament decided that the colonists should pay for the protection of their own lands, so they charged new taxes and restricted with whom the colonists could trade. Because the colonists did not have a Member of Parliament to represent them like other British subjects did, the colonists argued there should be "no taxation without representation."

In 1767, the Townshend Acts imposed taxes on items like tea, paper, and glass, and the revenue was used to pay for the salaries of government officials. Colonists were outraged, and a conflict broke out in Boston between British soldiers and a mob of colonists on March 5, 1770, now known infamously as the *Boston Massacre*. In response, Britain eliminated the taxes, but instituted a new tea tax. This led to the *Boston Tea Party* in December 1773, in which colonists dressed like Native Americans tossed tea arriving on British ships into the harbor. After many conflicts between Britain and the colonists, the *First Continental Congress* met in Philadelphia, Pennsylvania. Fifty-six representatives—for all colonies except Georgia—drafted the Declaration of Rights. A few British statesmen were sympathetic to the cause, including William Pitt (who would become British Prime Minister), but overall Parliament decided not to recognize their Declaration of Rights. On April 19, 1775, after British troops were sent to Lexington, Massachusetts, fighting broke out. The colonists were armed and ready, and the Revolution was underway.

In May 1775, the *Second Continental Congress* met in Philadelphia. George Washington (1732-1799) was made commander of the colonial armies. A year of fighting resulted in the *Declaration of Independence* on July 4, 1776. The conflict ended with the signing of a peace treaty in 1783, when Britain recognized America as a sovereign nation.

Many colonists—though not all—believed it was their moral duty as Christians to oppose the British. The only minister to sign the Declaration of Independence was John Witherspoon (1723-1794), president of The College of New Jersey (an Evangelical school later renamed Princeton). The Congress appointed him as a representative of New Jersey. When some argued that the colonies were not ready for independence, Witherspoon is known to have replied that it "was not only ripe for the measure, but in danger of rotting for the want of it."

Other Christians were not so eager for the Revolution. Anglican colonists, members of the official Church of England, found that their neighbors suspected their loyalties, so many went back to Britain. Some Methodists in America also returned to England in protest of the war, while others like Methodist Bishop Francis Asbury (1745-1816), a missionary sent to America by John Wesley, settled in the new country and became citizens.

Despite the varied role religion played in the American Revolution, in 1791, the Establishment Clause was added to the *Constitution of the United States*. It reads: "Congress shall make no law respecting an establishment of religion, or prohibiting the free exercise thereof." This statement allowed for freedom of religion and put the responsibility of religion on individuals and churches, rather than the government.

THE FRENCH REVOLUTION

From 1789-1799, France was turned upside down in a revolution. Among the many causes of the *French Revolution* was the inequitable *feudal system*. Centuries earlier the Reformation had seen an end to the feudal system in many countries, but it had lingered in France. There were three classes of people: the nobles, the clergy, and the commoners, each led by *Estates*. The nobles and the clergy did not pay taxes and had more privileges than the commoners, which the commoners resented. The French had also aided the colonists in the American Revolution, and because of war debts suffered financial instability. All of this led to a meeting of the three estates called the "Estates General" on May 5, 1789, in Versailles.

Most of the commoners (or Third Estate) broke off and formed a *National Assembly*, demanding reforms and opposing King Louis XVI. They wrote a constitution and made General Lafayette (whose army joined the Americans in their revolution) the leader of the new army. On August 26, 1789, the National Assembly, with the support of rioting commoners, ended feudalism by issuing the *Declaration of the Rights of Man and of the Citizen*. After further struggle and the capture of King Louis and Queen Marie Antoinette, France became a republic and the National Assembly became known as the *National Convention*. A decade of internal instability and economic failures followed, and then Napoleon Bonaparte (1769-1821) ended the Revolution by marching into Paris and naming himself "first consul" in 1799 and then emperor of France in 1804.

What did this mean for religion? Under the influence of Enlightenment thinkers, laws were instituted to reduce the church's power and to keep it out of political decisions. While Roman Catholicism remained the dominant religion in France, religious freedom was granted to the people in 1795.

TAIPING REBELLION

During the centuries of the rule of the Qing Dynasty (1644-1911), Christianity was banned in China. Many people saw the Qing Dynasty as corrupt. So in 1850 when a young leader named Hong Xiuquan (1814-1864) emerged with a call to reform China, many people were ready to follow him. This led to a conflict known as the *Taiping Rebellion*.

After failing his civil service exams several times, Hong believed he had a series of visions in which God called him to establish the Heavenly Kingdom of Great Peace (Taiping Tian Guo) on earth with himself as king. He called himself the son of God, by which he meant he was the new Messiah and a younger brother of Jesus Christ. He argued that everyone should share all their belongings in common, appealing to the general population. Other elements of Hong's beliefs come from his radical misreading of a tract written by China's first Protestant pastor, Liang Fa (1789-1855), called *Good Words to Admonish the Age*. Liang Fa was a convert of Robert Morrison (1782-1834), the first Evangelical Protestant missionary to China.

Hong's followers grew from a few thousand people to over

a million. He led his army in a revolt that almost overthrew the Qing government. The death toll of the civil war is estimated to be more than twenty million people. In 1864, the city of Nanking, which had been captured by the Taiping army, was recaptured by the government. Hong committed suicide.

The Taiping Rebellion made the progress of peaceful Christianity in China even more difficult. It gave greater reason for the Chinese government to resist Christian missionaries.

CHRISTIAN RESPONSES

Serious Christians looked to the Bible to decide how to respond to each of these revolutions, but they did not all agree on which side was right. One thing they all learned is that because the world is always changing, Christians always have the privilege of finding new ways to serve God in his world.

LIANG FA:
EVERYONE OUGHT TO KNOW

APRIL 1819. GULAO VILLAGE, GUANGDONG, CHINA.

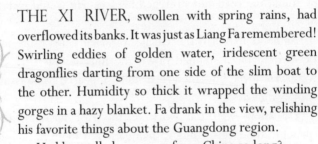

THE XI RIVER, swollen with spring rains, had overflowed its banks. It was just as Liang Fa remembered! Swirling eddies of golden water, iridescent green dragonflies darting from one side of the slim boat to the other. Humidity so thick it wrapped the winding gorges in a hazy blanket. Fa drank in the view, relishing his favorite things about the Guangdong region.

Had he really been away from China so long?

It was the poverty that had driven him away. He had ventured out of his family's village into the northwest cities, looking for work. In the shadow of the red Piyun Tower rising above the walls of Zhaoqing, he earned a little money. But as he traveled, he lost it on gambling. He would have been ruined if he had not made an unusual friend during his wanderings. William Milne, a printer from England, offered him a job carving blocks for his printing press. The job was in Malaysia, in the city of Malacca, a long way from home. But he needed steady work, so he took it.

And he was glad he did! It turned out that his new friend,

Milne, worked with a missionary named Robert Morrison, and the books they printed were about Jesus. The two men had been sent to China by the London Missionary Society, but the Chinese government had banned their work. So they set up their printing press in Malaysia and preached to Chinese people overseas. As Fa carved the blocks of words to be inked in the press, he read of Jesus' death and resurrection and his promise to come again.

Fa believed. And he learned from the missionaries how to follow Jesus. But now the time had come for him to leave the work there and return home. He was thirty years old and soon to be married.

He exited the small boat and paid the captain his fare. They had traveled up the Xi from the South China Sea and he was stiff from sitting all day in the wooden boat. Not far from the landing, he found the road and stretched his legs. He would walk the rest of the way.

As he approached the village, the rice fields came into view. Leveled terraces stepped down the hillside, each flooded with water. He loved how the green stalks appeared to be rising out of copper mirrors.

He knew well the work of the rice farmers. They first sprouted the rice seedlings, then gathered them in bundles to be transplanted into the paddies. The paddies were flooded to keep weeds from overtaking the crop. As a child, Fa loved to help with the transplanting. It was back breaking, but the intense heat didn't bother him with his feet in the cool water. He would roll up his baggy pant legs and tie them up under his tunic, then wade in ankle deep with a bundle of seedlings. He would tuck one plant into the saturated earth, then take a step backwards in the water and plant another. Plant a seedling, step back, plant a seedling, step back. With many workers, the paddy could be planted in one day.

When the crop was ready for harvest, they used a chain pump to drain out the water. After the paddy had sun-dried, his mother sent him out with a sickle. The stalks were bent with the weight of the rice. One swift swing and the fresh-cut bundle fell into his waiting arm.

His favorite part was the threshing floor. He loved beating the stalks, loading up a basket, and tossing it into the air. The wind carried away the empty husks while the heavy grains fell back to the mat at his feet.

It had been many years since he had planted or harvested rice. His hands were no longer calloused from the handle of the sickle. Instead, they were stained with inks used on the printing press.

Fa reached the village, where one bamboo roof after another ascended the hillside. It was the end of the day, and he smelled food drifting out of the houses as he climbed the steep dirt streets. "Mmm, that smells like roast duck," he thought. "And over here, oysters, eels. Maybe mushrooms?" His stomach growled. The night before, he had camped out on the bank of the Xi where he caught some frogs and cooked them over his small fire. But today he had eaten very little.

Just as he neared his parents' house, he saw a small woman carrying a wide basket. "Mother!" he shouted. "Mother!" But she did not look up. "Her hearing must not be so good now," he realized. He reached her and tapped her on the shoulder.

Startled, she spun around. Her basket hit the road, wobbling. He snatched it up before her day's worth of vegetable shopping tumbled out.

He took her face in his hands. "Mother, it's me, Fa."

She squinted at him with milky eyes. She had aged so much while he was gone! The deep wrinkles nearly hid her features. He leaned closer so she could make out his face.

Then the wrinkles broke into a toothless grin and she grabbed his cheeks with both her hands. "My son!" she cried.

"Yes, it is me."

"I did not know which day to expect you," she said. "You look well! You are strong, your clothing is not worn out. You have made money?"

"Yes, enough to keep myself fed." But his stomach disagreed and growled loudly.

She patted his belly. "Come in. I will serve you dinner." She pulled him into the house.

The main room was dim, lit only by two small windows. A cooking stove, stacked with pots, and a worktable filled one corner. Further back, floor-length curtains divided the sleeping areas.

Fa left his shoes at the door and put on a pair of black slippers. He rinsed his hands in the washbowl, then sat on a carpet in front of a low table. His mother put a bowl of steaming rice and three eggrolls in front of him, and poured tea into a smaller bowl.

"Thank you," he said. He raised the bowl of rice to his mouth and used chopsticks to push it quickly into his mouth. Not a single grain was left in the bowl when he set it back down.

A curtain at the back parted, and his father entered. He, too, looked much older than when Fa had last seen him. His shoulders were stooped from long years of bending over the rice paddies, and beneath his chin his long whiskers had turned white.

Fa jumped to his feet in respect. But his father took one look at him, turned around, and went back out as he had come in. Ever since Fa had left home to seek his fortune, his father had turned bitter against him. He would ignore his son for the first few days of each visit and then only grudgingly acknowledge his presence.

"Father!" he called out. But the curtain didn't move. Fa looked at his mother, hoping she would do something, but she just turned away.

That night he went out to watch the sun set. The ball of fire always seemed bigger falling behind the rooftops of his village than it did anywhere else. He suddenly wondered what his future bride, Li-Shi, would think of this little village tucked between the terraced rice fields. His parents had arranged his marriage years earlier. He had never met Li-Shi, and wouldn't until their wedding at the ancestral temple.

He went to bed that night thinking of how he could tell his family and his bride about the religion of Jesus.

Fa had his own tiny room in the back of the house, separated by a curtain. Now that he had returned, he went back to working with his parents in the fields and eating dinner with them after dark. But being home felt more like being in a foreign land. His parents went to the temple where he used to worship, but he only watched from a distance.

"Not long ago, I, too, was ignorant of the truth," he thought. When he was a child, he was taught the ideas of the philosopher Confucius. Fa had chosen an immoral life which was condemned by the teachings of Confucius, so in Malacca, when he desperately needed a new life, he turned for relief to the temples of Buddha.

His favorite was the temple of Kuan-Yin. Commoners and rich people came to this temple. The rich ones proudly wore their best robes, lighting incense and paying large amounts of money to the temple to be blessed. Fa never had a lot of money, so the priests told him to meditate.

The golden statue of Kuan-Yin seemed to stare back at him as he meditated. She sat cross-legged, her right hand forming the *mudra,* a sign that this was a temple of Buddhist teaching. Her other hand held a reddish-orange jewel representing the purity of the Buddha's teaching. Her throne was a lotus flower, a sacred symbol. The ability of the stem to rise above the mud and produce a delicate bloom was like the Buddhist's ability to rise above impurity to perfection. So they taught.

Fa desperately wanted to rise above his impurity. He thought, like the lotus flower, it was something he could achieve by himself if he tried hard enough. But working over the printing press making books about Jesus, he discovered he was wrong.

"Mr. Morrison and Mr. Milne showed me that only Christ's

sacrifice could make me pure," Fa remembered as he watched his parents make their daily visits to the temple. He wondered how he could help his family understand.

Soon everything was set for the wedding day. According to their traditions, his parents agreed to accept the dowry Li-Shi's parents could provide. In turn, they agreed to pay Li-Shi's parents a yearly sum for the cost of raising a girl.

The day before the wedding, Fa watched his father leave home by himself. He followed him to their ancestral temple. Fa knew his father was there to offer a sacrifice.

"He is asking for mercy upon me and my bride, and asking for our protection," he realized with a smile. He did not like to see his father worship an idol, but at least he knew that his father still loved him enough to care about his future. "I must do something to bring my father and the people of my village to Christ," he thought.

The next day, Fa entered the family temple for the first time since he had returned to China. His parents were there. Another older couple was there and a young woman draped in silk, with shining black hair knotted on top of her head. It was Li-Shi, his bride. They were not introduced, but the priest brought them together and pronounced a blessing on their marriage.

After the wedding, Li-Shi was carried in a covered chair to Fa's family home where they would live with his parents. She tried to hide the tears in her eyes as she left her parents' home for good. She knew it might be many years before she saw them again.

Their first few days together, Fa told his wife about his ancestors, the village of Gulao, and his life as a rice farmer and a printer's assistant. Li-Shi told him about the history of her family and her own village. She was kind and beautiful and worked hard to be a good daughter-in-law for Fa's parents. He decided they were a good match.

It was customary for a new bride to join her husband's family at their temple to call upon the ancestors for aid, and Li-Shi expected to do it. So it surprised her when Fa took her aside instead and showed her a black book.

"It's called the Bible," he said to her. "It is like our sacred texts, but this one tells us about Jesus, the Christ."

He held out the book to Li-Shi. She hesitated to take it, but she did not want to offend her new husband. So she opened it. Her eyebrows drew together in confusion as she read a small section of the New Testament.

Fa began to explain it to her. He told her about Jesus and the one God of the Christians who is not made of stone or wood, but is spirit. He told her that someday everyone's body would be resurrected, so there can be no such thing as reincarnation like the Buddhists teach.

She did not say a word, even when he asked her what she thought.

"She is afraid of leaving the religion of her family," he realized. "I cannot force her to change. I'll just have to talk about it from time to time and be patient."

Fa decided to begin the work of printing literature so his people could read about Jesus. He collected the best wood he could find. Then he went through his bags and pulled out the carving knives he had brought back from Malaysia. Huddled in his little corner of the house, he began carving wood blocks with quotes from the Bible. When he wasn't sure what to carve, he looked at the portions of the Bible his friend Robert Morrison had translated. The passages on idolatry seemed like a good place to start.

At night, Li-Shi poured tea and watched him work. Without getting in the way, she tried to catch glimpses of the text as he carved.

When he had completed a batch of printing blocks, he went to the street market to buy inks and paper. Soon he was inking the blocks and pressing them onto sheets of paper to bind together in a book. The smell of the inks drifted out into the street.

While Fa was out of the house, his father tried to read the blocks. Fa caught him doing this once and his father quickly left the house, shaking his head in disappointment. The smell of the ink was so strong inside, and he could tell his work upset his father, so he decided to build a booth off the back of the house where he could do his printing instead.

The day came when Fa carted a basket of his hand-printed books to a spot near the temple. After spending a few minutes in prayer, he stood at the side of the road, opened his Bible, and began preaching to the people passing by. Many of them just looked at him like he was crazy. But some stopped for a minute to hear his message, and even picked up some of his booklets. A few copies ended up in the muddy ditch, but he was encouraged to see some people reading them as they walked home.

That night, as he printed more books in his booth outside, his father appeared at the door. He was angry.

"Are you trying to disgrace your family?" he demanded, pointing to a stack of finished booklets.

Fa was puzzled. "Why would you say that?"

"I heard you were passing these out near the temple today. You turn your back on our religion and customs for the god of a foreigner? Were not the teachings of Confucius good enough for you?"

"I have learned much from our religion," said Fa. "I have learned about the importance of living a moral life. But Jesus tells me that no one can be good unless Jesus makes them good with his own perfection."

"I do not like this religion you teach. We know how to live the right life."

"The right life Confucius taught is just about external actions. Those actions do not change who I am inside. Jesus has done that."

His father tossed his hands in the air in disbelief. "They have confused your mind!" he said, and shuffled away.

Fa spent that evening praying again for his family to come to Christ.

The next day, he went back to the temple. Some of the temple worshipers who had taken booklets the day before came back and began asking him questions.

A young man came up to him. He was dressed in a coarse tunic and baggy pants and had a brimless black cap on his head. And he was carrying one of Fa's booklets in his hand, already folded and worn. "My name is Woo," he said with a traditional bow of greeting.

Fa bowed back. "Hello. I see you have read my booklet."

"Yes. I would like to know more about this Christ you teach. Can we go somewhere and talk?"

They walked to a quieter place away from the temple. Fa invited him to sit with him while he told him about his missionary friends.

"Do they live in the village?" Woo wanted to know. "I have never met this Morrison and Milne."

"No, they are in Malacca. Our government does not allow them to print their messages in our land."

"Yet you do it? Isn't it dangerous?"

"Everyone ought to know the saving doctrines," insisted Fa. "I do what I must for the people I love."

Woo tapped a dirty fingernail on the cover of the booklet. "This says there is forgiveness in Jesus, and that the gods are merely idols incapable of helping me. Is that true?"

"Certainly true."

"How do you know this?"

"I've found freedom and love in Jesus."

"But how do you know our gods are false?"

"Are they not just made of wood and stone?" was Fa's reply. "Do they not burn and break?"

"Yes."

"Jesus is different. He was resurrected from the dead. Even death had no power over him!"

Woo was quiet, and then said, "I want to think about this some more. Do you have other booklets? I will read whatever you have."

"Of course," Fa agreed. "And perhaps we can meet again tomorrow so I may answer any new questions you have."

"Thank you. You have made me curious about the Jesus god."

Fa went home that night wondering with excitement if Woo might be his first convert.

As weeks and months passed, Fa continued to preach and hand out booklets on the road to the temple. Attendance at the temple began to decline. Some worshipers were interested in Fa's message and came to hear him speak instead of going into the temple. Others did not want to have to pass him on their way in, for fear he would start to debate them, so they simply decided to stay home from the temple.

The temple priests became more and more concerned about the crazy man who was distracting the people from worship. So they told the police that Fa was starting a revolution.

One morning before dawn, Fa was asleep on his mat next to his wife when a sudden shouting of voices jolted him awake. The curtain was torn aside. Li-Shi screamed and tried to hide under the blanket. Fa rubbed his eyes and when they focused saw two officers standing over him.

"Get up," an officer shouted.

Fa stumbled from his mat, reaching for his shirt, but the officer grabbed his arm and slapped him across the face.

Li-Shi screamed again.

"Are you Liang Fa?" demanded the officer.

"Yes, I am. What is going on?"

"You're coming with us." The policemen dragged him toward

the door and out onto the street. "Keep moving!" they shouted, prodding him with a sharp bamboo stick.

They forced him behind the house. Fa watched as they ripped up his printing booth and dumped all his woodblocks, knives, inks, and papers into a cart. Then they tossed him in the cart, too.

As the cart carried them down the steep road Fa looked back and saw all the neighbors' lamps were lit. Their faces stared at him from out of their windows. He hadn't had time to get dressed and here he was being carted away in public! As the cart flew around a corner, Fa's last glimpse was of his father stooped over in the damaged doorway, his head hung with shame.

The long bumpy cart ride ended at the Guangdong court house. Down a dark hallway with drops of humidity clinging to the walls, the policemen dragged him into a cell. It was already occupied by several prisoners crammed together on one worn mat.

The officer had Fa's shirt and threw it at him. "Put this on. They don't want to see you naked."

The other prisoners mocked him, happy for any form of entertainment.

Fa quickly drew the garment over his head and heard the cell door slam. "Wait—!" he cried. But the officers were gone.

"You are Liang Fa," said a voice.

Fa looked up to see a tall man standing in the darkness at the back of the cell. From his appearance, he had been in prison for a while.

"How do you know me?" said Fa, trembling.

"You are the one they say is disturbing the peace in Gulao Village." The man looked him up and down and then snorted. "But you are thin and frail. You are no threat."

"Of course I am not a threat," said Fa. "I am preaching the message of Jesus Christ."

"I have heard of this Jesus. A Christian once told me about him. But we do not need the foreigners' god." The man leaned uncomfortably close to Fa's face. "Why don't you call on your god to get you out of this prison?"

Fa crossed his arms. "I am already a free man. I've been set free from my sin."

"As free as a prisoner!" the man bellowed, striking the wall with his fist.

The other prisoners laughed.

Fa had no time to respond because the cell door swung open again. "Liang Fa, come with us."

The prisoner peered at Fa again and whispered, "If you don't like pain, I suggest you start calling upon your Jesus."

The officers took Fa down the hallway again and into a small room where a man was waiting for him. He told him to sit at the table, and Fa's throat caught when he saw it was covered with dried spatters of blood. It was also piled with woodblocks and booklets.

"Are these yours?" the man began, his voice strangely polite.

Fa looked with sorrow on the pile of booklets. They had taken so many hours to print.

"The words in this book are the religion of foreigners in our land," the man said when Fa didn't reply. "They are not welcome here and are forbidden by law."

Still Fa said nothing.

"I asked you if these are yours!" the interrogator yelled. He leaped forward and swung his fist firmly into Fa's nose.

The blow knocked Fa out of his seat. "They are mine," he cried, tasting salty blood on his lips.

"Get back into your seat." The man's voice was calm again.

Fa crawled back into the chair.

"What is your purpose with these? Are you trying to lead a rebellion?"

"No!"

"Then why have you come here with your rebellious writings?"

"I was born here in Gulao. I want to give my friends and family the good news."

"What good news?"

"The good news of forgiveness. The ability to live a right life through Jesus Christ."

The interrogator put both hands on the table. "This is a lie," he said, his voice rising. "You are trying to stir up the people."

Fa shook his head. "No, I'm telling the truth!"

"I do not tolerate liars!" the man shouted, jumping up again. This time he pulled out a thick bamboo stick and beat Fa across the shoulder, knocking him to the floor again.

"I am telling the truth," Fa whimpered from the floor.

"Take him back to his cell," the man ordered his officers. "We will give him time to re-think his position."

They shoved him into the cell again. Fa squatted in the corner, holding his shirt to his nose to stop the bleeding.

"I see they've given you a good welcome," said the tall prisoner. "It only gets worse from here."

Fa groaned. "They believe I am trying to stir up the people in a revolt."

"Are you?"

"No!"

"I would not try to hide it. If you are, they will find out." He snapped his fingers at the other prisoners, who immediately crammed together to make room for Fa on the edge of the mat.

"Thank you." Fa winced as he laid down on the mat.

"And even if you aren't, they will make up evidence that says you are."

"That is immoral," said Fa, his voice muffled by the mat. "Even Confucius would condemn them."

"Forget Confucius and sleep," the man said, withdrawing to his corner. "They will be back for you."

Fa shut his eyes, trying to block out the pain in his swelling nose and throbbing shoulder. But he couldn't sleep. "Maybe I shouldn't have disobeyed the law," he thought. "Maybe I shouldn't have stood so close to the temple. But how else can I tell my people about Jesus?" He wished Mr. Milne and Mr. Morrison were there to give him advice.

In the morning the officers came again and put Fa in the secluded room. "What are these books?" the interrogator asked again, as if he expected a different answer. "What is their purpose?"

"They tell of the loving message of Jesus," said Fa without hesitation. He had already learned that keeping silent led to more pain. "It is what I told you yesterday. Nothing has changed since then."

"These ideas are not allowed in Guangdong. Your missionary friends cannot preach here so they send you? They are cowards."

"No," Fa insisted. "I came here because it was time for me to marry."

"Did you bring these books with you?"

"Not these," said Fa. "I made these here."

"You did this by yourself?"

"Yes."

"You are lying! You are here to help these foreigners stir up your village!" He pulled out the bamboo rod and beat Fa across his face and stomach. Then he grabbed his head and forced him to look out the tiny window.

Outside the courthouse, officers were dumping his woodblocks and piles of booklets into a bonfire. Smoke brought the smell of burning ink to his nostrils. He sagged with despair, but before the interrogator shoved him away from the window, he caught a glimpse of Woo near the fire. Woo was weeping as the charred scraps floated up from the flames.

Fa's days became a loop of questioning, torture, and collapsing on the floor of his cell. Every morning they yanked him out and demanded to know about the uprising he was planning. He always told them the same thing, that he was spreading a message of peace in Christ. With each beating, he wished he had learned more from the missionaries. He wondered if he would ever see Li-Shi again.

"Tell them you came to start an uprising," his tall cellmate advised him. "They will you kill you quickly and put an end to your torture."

But Fa refused. "I cannot betray Christ."

"Clearly he has betrayed you," said his friend.

But one morning, the officers did not take him to the torture room. Instead, they pushed him toward the door.

"You must have important friends," said one. "Several merchants connected to the foreigner Morrison have contacted the magistrate to demand your release."

Fa spun around. His nose was still swollen between two black eyes, but he was smiling ear to ear. "I'm free?" he cried.

"Do not smile too quickly. You are to be released, but not until you pay the price for breaking the law."

Outside, they stripped off his clothes and strapped his arms to two poles. "This will teach you not to disrupt the peace," said the officer.

At his signal, a big man stepped forward. He carried a whip of sturdy bamboo that was almost as long as Fa was tall.

Fa shut his eyes. The cane struck the backs of his legs with a stinging crack. After thirty blows, blood was running down between his toes. He stumbled when they released his wrists from the straps and fell when they shoved him out to the street.

"Do not preach your message again!" they shouted, and threw his blood-stained clothes at him.

He lay in the street with his face in the dust, trying to summon the strength to get up. Then a friendly voice said, "Here, Fa, let me help you." He looked up to see Woo standing over him.

The boy bent down and helped him up by the shoulders. "I have a cart," he said. "I'll get you back to your family."

Fa grasped Woo's hand. "Thank you, my friend. How did you get me released? Did you contact the missionaries?"

Woo shook his head. "It wasn't me. I tried to get word to the missionaries in Malacca, but I didn't know how to reach them. And then I found out they had already heard and were making arrangements for your release. They asked me to give you the message that they want you to come back and learn more with them."

"I want to," said Fa. "I don't think I am very good yet at being a missionary!"

Woo got him into the cart and took him back to the village. His father would not come out from behind his curtain, and his mother just cried at the sight of his face and legs. In their private sleeping area, Li-Shi cleaned the blood from his wounds. He winced as she applied a smelly ointment to the cuts and bruises. When she had tied the last of the bandages, he took her small hands in his own.

"Li-Shi, I did not mean to disgrace you."

She lowered her gaze. "I know. You believe your religion and you love your people."

"Yes, I do. And that is why I must go back to Malacca soon. I should not be seen for a while, and I want to be trained by Mr. Morrison on how to better evangelize my people." He waited until she looked at him. "Li-Shi, would you be pleased to come with me?"

She was quiet for a moment, and then shook her head. "I have already left my village, Fa. I do not wish to leave China, too. And without you, your parents must work harder with the crops. I will stay and help them."

He saw that she was sincere. "As you wish," he said.

She got up to get him fresh clothes, and when she came back with them he was holding out a book to her. It was the little black Bible he had showed her after their wedding. "I am leaving this with you. It is the most important book in the world, Li-Shi. I would be very happy if you would read it while I'm gone."

"Since it means so much to you, I will," she said, and tucked it under the mat.

With Li-Shi's strong ointment, the wounds on his legs healed quickly. When the morning of his departure arrived, he kissed his wife goodbye. He would not have to hunt for frogs on his journey because his mother had wrapped up some rice and mushrooms and a slice of his favorite roast duck. And though his father said nothing, he walked with him as far as the rice paddies.

Fa went on alone. He looked back once, turning on the road to memorize the terraced fields and the jumble of roofs that made up his beloved Gulao. Then he set his face toward the sun and made his way down to the banks of the Xi to catch a boat back to the South China Sea.

Liang Fa returned to Malaysia to be discipled by Robert Morrison and William Milne. Milne died in 1822. The following year Morrison, the first Protestant missionary to China, ordained Fa as the first Protestant Chinese evangelist and pastor. Supported by the London Missionary Society, he returned to China. He helped to distribute the Morrison-Milne Bible translation throughout China, and wrote several books, including a commentary on Hebrews. Because Christianity remained illegal in China, he was forced to flee for his life on more than one occasion. One of Fa's students later led a movement that initiated the bloody Taiping Rebellion, which Fa opposed.

His wife Li-Shi became a Christian and was baptized in 1820. Fa's father continued to reject the gospel, but never disowned his son.

In 1855, at the age of 66, Fa died and was buried in his ancestral cemetery in Guangdong province.

A New Method of Missions

IN THE EIGHTEENTH and nineteenth centuries, Christians across the world were engaged in missionary work. The development of modern missions became one of the most important contributions to the gospel that came out of the First and Second Great Awakenings.

Christian missionaries were not new, of course. From the time of the Apostle Paul until the present, Christians have carried the gospel into the world to fulfill the *Great Commission* Jesus gave in Matthew 28:19 to "go and make disciples of all nations, baptizing them in the name of the Father and of the Son and of the Holy Spirit." But with the discovery of new lands and new trade routes came new missions opportunities for Christians. And as they took notes and formed support organizations, they began to learn better ways to engage in their work.

EARLY NATIVE AMERICAN MISSIONS
In the middle of the seventeenth century, John Eliot (1604-1690)

was a missionary to the Native Americans of Massachusetts. He believed one of the first tasks of a missionary is to put the Bible into the hands of the people, so he translated the Bible into the native Algonquian language. He also taught his converts to become evangelists of their own people instead of relying on outsiders to do it. Eliot made these and other advances in missionary principles, but he still expected his converts to dress in English clothing once they converted instead of retaining their cultural identity. There was still a lot of progress to be made on the mission field.

Mission work among Native Americans became a special focus of North American missionaries, especially Evangelicals. One of these was David Brainerd (1718-1747), a Presbyterian who ministered to the Seneca and Delaware Indians of New York, New Jersey, and Pennsylvania in the 1740s. When Brainerd died of tuberculosis at the home of Jonathan Edwards, Edwards published Brainerd's diary. *The Life of David Brainerd* (1749) became a bestseller and encouraged generations of missionaries to go into missions. When Jonathan Edwards left his Northampton church in 1751, he moved to the mission outpost of Stockbridge, Massachusetts and ministered to Mohican and Mohawk families.

THE START OF MISSIONARY SOCIETIES

Evangelical missionary William Carey (1761-1834) was also moved by the life of Brainerd. In 1792 he published a book calling for Christians to engage whole-heartedly in international missions. Carey and others founded the Baptist Missionary Society and Carey went to India to put his convictions into action.

Sometimes missionaries worked with their governments to get funding for overseas missions. This did not always work out well. There were times when their governments used them for strategic political gain, and even restricted their work. One of the worst results of such policies is that it could be difficult for missionaries to win the trust of the locals to whom they ministered, since people suspected them of spying. Many missionaries went on their own or at the request of a missionary society to avoid these problems. Others began with a missionary society and eventually withdrew, surviving as part of a missionary community in which each person pulled his or her own weight to make it work.

Besides Carey's Baptist Missionary Society, other Evangelical mission societies formed around the same time, such as the London Missionary Society (1795) and the American Baptist Foreign Missions Society (1814). The London Missionary Society sent Presbyterian missionary Robert Morrison to southern China, making him the first Protestant Missionary there. Morrison's convert Liang Fa became the first Chinese pastor ordained by the London Missionary Society. They found that mission work was more effectively done by people native to the land. Adoniram (1788-1850) and Ann (1789-1826) Judson helped to found the American Baptist Foreign Missions Society and went to the mostly hostile country of Burma. They tried various techniques to reach out to the people, but were unsuccessful until they built a traditional shelter the Burmese people used for resting and discussing religion. Then the people came and heard the gospel.

David Livingstone (1813-1873) was a missionary-explorer, venturing across the African continent to preach the gospel and record everything he learned about the cultures. He saw his job as not only paving the way for missions, but also for commerce that would provide income for the poorest Africans. He worked first with a mission agency and later with the British government.

Hudson Taylor (1832-1905) formed the China Inland Mission in 1865. He was dedicated to presenting the pure gospel, without the added elements of Western culture, and was known for dressing and living like the Chinese people he served.

MISSIONARY TRAINING

As more missionaries reported back what they were learning from their efforts, special missionary training schools were formed. One of these was Andover Seminary, which Adoniram Judson's father helped to found and where Adoniram studied after college. Another was Mount Holyoke Female Seminary, founded by Mary Lyon (1797-1849), where many women were trained for the mission field, including Fidelia Fiske (1816-1864), missionary to present-day Iran. The Massachusetts school was known for some of the most aggressive missionary efforts of the day.

The work of missions is performed by Christians of all backgrounds in every country today. But during the time of the Great Awakenings, Evangelical missionaries labored to the death to bring the gospel to new lands while respecting the local cultures. And they recorded their efforts so later missionaries could learn from their mistakes and successes. By trial and error, they developed modern foreign missions.

Ad⊕niram and Ann Jud⊕on:
I bear in my b⊕dy

FEBRUARY 1824. AVA, THE CAPITAL CITY OF BURMA.

CRATES AND TRUNKS piled up on the verandah as willing hands carted them up the stairs. Ann could not unpack them as fast as her husband Adoniram and their assistant Moung Ing delivered them. Though it was the cool season in Burma, the work made her perspire, and she decided to take a break on the porch.

Adoniram had obviously had the same thought. He was leaning against the rail, his face turned into the breeze, when she stepped outside.

The house was raised four feet off the ground by stilts, a necessity during heavy rains. It was made of bamboo and wood planks, and consisted of just three small rooms and a verandah. Their families back home would never have considered it luxurious, but she thought it comfortable. The view was pleasant, taking in the sandy slope toward lush vegetation on the riverbank. An opening in the trees offered a glimpse of the coppery water.

"I still cannot believe we built this house in only two weeks," said Ann, breaking the silence.

Her husband nodded. "But I wish we'd had time to get bricks."

"I know. This wooden box will be an oven in another two months. Still, it is far better than Dr. Price's damp house, and roomier than the boat we've been living on for the last few weeks."

"Well, as soon as I can acquire enough bricks, we'll start on permanent buildings for the mission." He pointed to the left. "Our house will go over there. And the *zayat* where we will preach will be there. And then the schoolroom and clinic that way."

Ann studied his profile as he talked, marveling at his energy after the long journey to Ava and the work of constructing the house. A decade in the Burmese sun had tanned his skin, but he was still young and strong. "Though I think his hair receded while I was away," she thought, and she noted some streaks of gray.

Their months of separation while she was in the States for medical treatment had been hard on both of them. They had always been a close team, relying on each other's talents and encouragement. They were both from Massachusetts. When they met, she was teaching school there and he was finishing a degree at Andover Seminary, the pastoral training school his father had helped start based on the teachings of Jonathan Edwards. She was impressed by the Brown University valedictorian who had recently dedicated his life to God. And he was just as taken by the smart, pretty woman who was convinced God wanted to use her on the foreign mission field. They were ordained the day after their wedding, and thirteen days later boarded a ship in Boston Harbor to sail to India.

In Serampore, they toured William Carey's mission and began language study. But they found themselves called to the neighboring country of Burma, and settled down to start a mission of their own in the town of Rangoon. Once Adoniram had learned the language well enough to preach, they built a *zayat*, a traditional meeting house where the locals came to get out of the heat, discuss religion, and read gospel tracts. Every Sunday, the Judsons held worship in their *zayat*. Ann translated the book of Matthew into

Thai, and the books of Daniel and Jonah into Burmese, and wrote a Burmese catechism. Adoniram started work on an English-Burmese dictionary and began translating the New Testament. At the end of ten years, ten locals had converted to Christianity and started preaching to their neighbors.

So with their tiny church flourishing in Rangoon, the Judsons accepted an invitation by the king of Burma to start a new mission in the capital city, Ava. Just days after Ann returned from medical treatment in the United States, they started on their six-week journey by boat up the Irawaddy River. After two more weeks of cutting down trees and tying bamboo to make the house, the new mission was starting to take shape.

Lost in her memories, Ann didn't notice Adoniram had fallen silent. He was gazing at her now, realizing that he had been so busy he hadn't really looked at her for awhile. She had pinned up her curly hair as she always did, but was it darker than it used to be? She said she was feeling much better after her treatment, but she seemed thinner and her face had lost the rosy blush of health. "I suppose the long return voyage sapped some of the strength she regained in the States," he thought.

But she turned and smiled up at him. "I'm looking forward to reading your New Testament translation," she said.

"Apparently you had to leave me for weeks in order for me to get it done!"

"I see. Well, glad I could help. Now what about the Old Testament?"

He laughed. "One thing at a time, my dear."

Two little Burmese girls, their black hair parted into glossy braids, stuck their heads out the door. "Mama, we have found a place for the box of hair ribbons you gave us," said the oldest.

"Good job," Ann said, squatting down to face them at eye level. "Now, go get the grammar book and help each other with your lesson until I come in with a new task for you. All right?"

"Yes, Mama!" They giggled and ran back inside.

"I am surprised at how quickly Mary and Abby have taken to you," Adoniram said with a look of admiration.

"They never had any affection or discipline from their mother, the poor deranged thing, and their father's employment was so uncertain. They are just happy to have regular meals and a bit of education. I'm very pleased with their studies."

"And their classmates?"

"The girls have each stitched their own aprons and are reading at various levels. The students are still few in number, but I expect an increase as the locals learn about my school."

"It will make a difference once you have a permanent building," he assured her.

She looked back toward the river, staring at the dark water on the other side of the trees. "Adoniram, do you think the king is still favorable to us?" she asked suddenly.

He put both hands on the rail, his shoulder next to hers. "The winds of politics have shifted lately with these rumors of war," he admitted. "The king received me last time I visited, but his advisors I met last year when I worked out the arrangements for this land are strangely gone now. And their replacements are not as friendly."

At her concerned look, he hurried on. "Still, we were promised protection. If they do end up at war with the British, the people here seem to understand that we're Americans, not Brits. We have no stake in their disagreements. So I think we'll be alright."

"I hope so." She pushed away from the rail. "Well, there is Moung Ing with another load from the boat. We still have a lot of work to do."

"Yes, we do! I'll help him with these crates so you can get the girls started on something else."

They went back to unpacking.

Within weeks, Adoniram was preaching in Burmese every Sunday at the home of their friend, Dr. Price, who lived downriver.

People came from all over the region, even the prince. On weekday evenings, some of the locals joined them in their home for Christian worship. Ann added a few students to her school.

They tried to stay optimistic, but the political situation was rapidly getting worse. One Sunday in May, they had just finished the service at Dr. Price's house when a messenger arrived with news that the British had taken Rangoon.

"What of our mission there?" cried Ann. "The native church will be fine, but our American colleagues there might be in danger."

The messenger could not tell them details. But Dr. Price was concerned. "The king knows we're not British, but some of our support does come from Christians in England. He could misinterpret that. We need to be careful."

The warm season arrived, and as the temperature rose, so did the tension. On a hot June night, the Judson household was preparing for dinner when they heard voices outside. A dozen Burmese soldiers, with a man they recognized as an executioner, barged into the house.

"Are you the teacher?" the officer demanded.

"Yes, I'm Adoniram Judson."

"You are being arrested by order of the king." The officer jerked his head at the executioner. "Take him."

"On what charge?" Adoniram cried. "I am here at the king's request and under his protection!"

The man shrugged. "You are a white man, and we are at war with Britain. You're probably spying for them!"

"No, I'm American! There must be some mistake."

The officer ignored his protest. The executioner threw Adoniram to the floor and began to tie his hands and feet with a cord. The Burmese servant, Moung Ing, shoved Mary and Abby behind him and looked at Ann for orders.

But she had run toward the officer. "Please, don't do this," she begged. "I will give you money."

The soldiers looked at each other, eager to supplement their pay with a bribe.

"Arrest her too," said the officer. "She is also a foreigner."

"No!" shouted Adoniram. "If the king did not order her arrest, you dare not touch her."

The officer nodded to the executioner to let her go. "Leave her for now. But you will be under guard, Mrs. Judson, until we find out what the king wants us to do with you."

They shoved Adoniram outside, where by this time people from the neighborhood had gathered. "Why are you taking him?" they were shouting in confusion. "He is no spy! He is just a teacher!"

The soldiers pushed past them and dragged their prisoner away.

Ann ran into her room and grabbed some silver out of a chest under the bed. Thrusting it into Moung Ing's hands, she told him to follow the soldiers and see where they were taking her husband. "If you can bribe anyone to let him go, do it," she said. "Tell them I have more, if necessary."

Without a word, he flew down the stairs. Ann saw that the officer had left two guards at her gate. She banged the door shut and barricaded it with a table. Taking the frightened girls by their little hands, she fled back into her room. On her knees, she begged God to keep her husband safe and give her wisdom.

Then she had a thought. She ran through the house, snatching up Adoniram's journals and letters. Anything that mentioned England she threw into her cookstove and set on fire. They were just simple requests for supplies and books, but clearly there were already too many misunderstandings. She couldn't risk any more.

She jumped at a bang on the door. "Mrs. Judson," a man called. "It's the magistrate. I have come to question you."

She stirred up the ashes in the stove to be sure everything was destroyed. With quiet words, she tucked the girls into her bed and told them to stay, then shut the bedroom door firmly.

"Mrs. Judson, you must let me in!"

She pushed the heavy table away from the door and stepped aside so the magistrate could come in. "Can I get you some tea?" she asked.

He stared at her. Her face was stained with tears, but she was calm. She reached for the kettle.

"No, thank you, Mrs. Judson. I'm sorry, but I must ask you some questions. Please sit."

She dropped into a chair across from him and he began to interrogate her. What was she doing in Burma? How long had they been there? Who did they know in Rangoon? Did they have friends in the British government?

Finally, he was convinced she was not a danger to the crown. He agreed to let her stay in her house, and promised that the guards outside were there to protect her.

But after he left, the guards began to harass her. They stood on the verandah and pounded on the door and walls to scare her. She could hear their laughter and coarse language. The girls were terrified.

"Leave us alone!" she cried through the wall. "Go away and let us sleep, and in the morning I will make you breakfast."

The soldiers went back down to the gate. Ann sank to the floor and waited for Moung Ing to return with news. When he did, it wasn't good. He hadn't been able to bribe the soldiers into releasing Adoniram. Worse, they had taken him to the prison known as Let-ma-yoon, which in Burmese means, "Hand, shrink not." It was a torture house.

Darkness was falling as Adoniram was dragged into the prison compound. His heart sank when he saw Dr. Price and several European businessmen he knew. They were all being carried in, each arrested in his home. The soldiers shoved them toward the enclosure's main building, a ramshackle square of bamboo with a sloping roof.

With a shove, Adoniram fell past the door into foul-smelling blackness. He gagged. The atmosphere inside was thick and intense, the heat unbearable. A smoky flame in a clay pot wavered from the top of a tripod in the middle of the room. As his eyes adjusted to the darkness, he could make out long shadows on the floor. The shapes became clearer and he realized he was looking at human bodies. At least eighty prisoners, men and women, shackled on their backs. Some were so thin he thought at first they were skeletons until they moaned, begging him for water.

"Move!" bellowed a soldier, and reinforced his command with a heavy club.

Adoniram was pushed forward with the other prisoners and knocked to his back with Dr. Price at his side. They locked his legs in weighted stocks, the heavy wood cutting into his ankles. He didn't want to know what substance was soaking through the back of his shirt. Staring up in the dark, he saw a long bamboo pole hanging from the ceiling by ropes at both ends.

"Price, what is that pole for?" he trembled.

"I think we are about to find out," Price groaned back.

He was right. They soon learned of the night watchman's favorite ritual. The pole was strung between the prisoners' legs and then hoisted into the air just high enough to leave only their heads and shoulders on the ground. The blood rushed out of their legs in a wave of dizziness. They would spend the night upside down, with the weight of the stocks bearing down on their shoulders, listening to colonies of rats scratch around them. Adoniram retreated into his mind and pictured his beautiful Ann.

Ann's first sleepless night ended at dawn, when she left the girls in Moung Ing's care, bribed the guards with tea and cigars, and walked several miles into the city to see the magistrate. He refused to hear her appeal.

She wrote a note to one of the king's sisters, a woman she had once met for tea, and pleaded with her to ask the king to release

Adoniram. But when the messenger returned, he said, "The lady does not understand what you wrote."

"Of course she understands!" Ann cried in anguish. "She must be afraid to get involved." Ann didn't know what else to do. She walked back home, praying the whole way.

Later, Moung Ing went out and quietly scoured the city for information. He reported that all the white men had been arrested for spying and that the king had not decided if he was going to execute them or not. Ann despaired for all their European friends.

In the morning, she sent a message to the governor, requesting an audience. To her surprise, he agreed. She nearly ran the whole way into the city and threw herself on his mercy.

"I wish I could help you, Mrs. Judson," he said, with genuine concern on his wrinkled old face. "But it is not within my power. I don't have the authority to release them."

The strain was too much for Ann. She began to cry. "Please, please, Governor! There must be something you can do!"

"Don't cry, my dear," he said, shifting uncomfortably. He glanced toward the door. "Look, I cannot release them," he said softly, "but I can make them more comfortable."

Ann looked up hopefully. "You can?"

The governor called over a lieutenant who was hovering in the doorway. "It is his job to oversee the prisons. He might be willing to, er, arrange for special conditions."

The officer took her aside. He did not look friendly to Ann, but she knew government officials lived by bribes. And this one could be of great assistance. "I am willing to help relieve your husband's pain," he said, "but I will need three hundred *rupees*, two lengths of broadcloth, and two handkerchiefs."

Ann's heart sank. "I can give you the money," she said, pulling her coin purse from her pocket, "but I don't have that type of cloth."

The officer looked at her through narrowed eyes. "Very well. I will do it for the money only. But you must speak directly to me about this arrangement and tell no one."

She nodded and handed him the money. He counted it quickly, tucked it in his pocket, and then nodded across the room to the governor.

The governor said nothing about the transaction, but gave Ann a written order allowing her to visit her husband in prison.

She ran to the prison, waving the governor's order at the guards behind the fence of sharpened bamboo poles. They brought her inside the gate, and told her to wait. She was dismayed at the state of the buildings, and shocked to see a starving tiger in a cage at the back of the enclosure. She shuddered to think why they kept it there.

The sagging door of the main cell opened, and they dragged Adoniram out. She cried out at the sight of him. "Oh, what have they done to you?"

In only two days, her usually spotless and unwrinkled husband had become a wretched, smelly creature. His shirt was gone, and his hair and body were coated with filth. He could barely walk.

He tried to speak, but his mouth was parched. She begged a guard to give him a little water.

"It will be all right," she said tearfully. "I have spoken to the governor, and he is going to help us."

"I'm so sorry you have to go through this," he said hoarsely.

"Me? No, darling, I am fine. Moung Ing is with me. But you! I'm going to get you out of here."

But the guards dragged him away again and forced her out.

That night, Moung Ing came back from his nightly investigation and reported that thanks to her payment, Adoniram and Dr. Price had been moved out of the common cell into a smaller, cleaner one away from the other prisoners. Ann was able to send them food and mats to sleep on. But they wouldn't let her visit again.

Her days of pleading with the governor and the magistrate and the queen turned into weeks. And then she discovered that the situation was even more complicated. Ann was pregnant!

She began to feel ill again, but refused to stop going to the prison everyday and bribing the guards to deliver food and other supplies to her husband. She was the only bright thing in the prison, and some of the guards began to look forward to her visits. She came even on the hottest days and during the weeks of heavy rains, her belly growing bigger all the time. As long as she kept coming with gifts for the guards, she was able to keep Adoniram out of the common prison where the conditions were the worst.

But it was inevitable that her visits would stop, temporarily. On a January morning, Moung Ing helped her give birth to little Maria. They were both ill and it was weeks before Ann was strong enough to get out of bed and make the several-mile walk to the prison. When she arrived, she discovered that the little cell built for Adoniram had been demolished. They had returned him to the common prison.

She marched to the governor's house and railed at him. "To this point, you have treated me with kindness," she began. "I looked to you for protection from oppression and cruelty, and you have helped alleviate the sufferings of those innocent people in your charge. You promised me you would stand by me. So why has Adoniram been moved back into the common prison to be tortured?"

The old governor turned away from Ann in shame. "For some reason, you stir pity in me like no one else. You must believe me when I tell you that I do not want to increase your husband's punishment. But, please understand! I have been ordered to execute the foreigners three times now, and each time I have hidden them to save their lives. I wish I could release your husband from his present confinement, but I cannot." He was weeping into his hands.

Ann believed him. She had never seen the man in such a state. Helpless, she slipped out the door and went home.

Weeks passed. One day, a bribe revealed that Adoniram had developed a high fever in his wretched cell. Desperate to get him medical attention, she left the house in Moung Ing's care. With Maria in her arms and Mary and Abby at her side, she built a bamboo tent outside the prison gate. She would stay there day and night until Adoniram was released.

The governor could not bear her daily pleading. He finally gave the order to let her into the prison to bring Adoniram medicine. The guards refused to let her enter the cell, but they dragged the sick man to the door so she could pour the medicine between his lips.

She touched his wasted body with tender hands. "My poor Adoniram," she murmured. "I wish I could do more for your wounds and your fever."

"The worst thing," he whispered, "is the idleness of my mind. All these days when I could be working on my Bible translation! I came here to work, Ann, to preach the gospel to the people, not to waste my life—and yours." He tried to moisten his lips. "How is the baby?"

"She is fine, darling," she called as they carried him inside again. "Don't worry—you will meet her soon!"

The guards saw that her medicines relieved his symptoms. They heard she had given her two adopted girls shots to keep them from getting smallpox. So they brought their children to get inoculated, too. She prayed with them and told them about Jesus, the Great Physician. And she asked them to help her get her husband released. It was not the way she had planned to deliver the gospel in Ava.

But yet another surprise awaited her. One day, when Ann returned with Maria to the bamboo tent from her visit to the governor, the girls told her Moung Ing had been looking for her. She ran after him.

He was frantic when he saw her. "Mrs. Judson, the prisoners are gone! I can't find them!"

They ran to the prison wall and shouted, but got no response. They ran to the place where prisoners were often executed, but found no bodies. With Maria crying in her arms, she stopped everyone on the street, begging for information. But no one would tell her anything. She flew back to the governor's house.

"I'm sorry," he said, hanging his head. "I knew they were to be removed, and I didn't want you to be in danger when the soldiers came to get them, so I kept you here."

"You deceived me!" she cried. Maria was wailing.

"I did not know they were to be moved until this morning. I have just learned that they are being sent to Oung-pen-la."

"Why?" demanded Ann. "Do not hide anything from me."

"I do not know. I am telling you the truth."

"Then I'll follow them and find out for myself!"

"Please," he begged her, his coppery forehead wrinkled with concern, "you have done all you could do for your husband. Now you must take care of yourself and your daughter."

She stumbled out the door in tears. At the tent, she collected Moung Ing and the girls, and they walked the long road back to the house on the river. She collapsed on her bed in exhaustion. After a few hours of sleep and another hour of prayer, she packed two trunks with the food and medicine they would need for a journey, and hired a boat.

They traveled to Oung-pen-la first by boat, then by hired cart. It was a whole day's journey with Maria in her arms and the girls and Moung Ing at her side. When the cart driver refused to continue on to the prison, they got out and walked the rest of the way.

The new prison yard was more distressing than the old one. The sagging building had no roof and only three sides. As she approached, she saw Adoniram and the others chained inside. She got as close as she could and held Maria up so he could see her.

But a look of pain crossed his face when he recognized them. "Why have you come?" he groaned. "It is not safe for you here!"

"I won't let them take you away from me!"

"What about our mission?"

"My work now is to care for you until we can return to our mission together." She held Maria tight against her chest and tried to get a closer look at her husband's condition. "What happened to your feet?"

"Blisters," he said, refusing to look down at the bloody wrappings. "Mr. Gouger's servant walked with us, and tore his turban in two to wrap up our miserable feet. They forced us to walk the whole way, and at the hottest time of day." He lowered his voice. "One of the men did not make it."

Ann tried to hold back her tears, but she was so tired and so afraid.

Adoniram struggled to sit up. "Ann, think of it this way. Now, like the Apostle Paul, I bear in my body the marks of the Lord Jesus!" He fell back. "And the comfort of your nearness is a mercy from him. A million men could not hope to have your strength."

"I won't leave Oung-pen-la until you do, too," she promised.

Night was falling, and she needed to find shelter. She asked one of the prison guards if she could put up a tent.

"No, no," he said, shaking his head. "It is not allowed, and it would not be safe."

"But I have nowhere else to go!" she insisted.

He looked down at the baby in her arms, and then said, "You may stay with my family. We have a second room."

He didn't mention that the second room was a grain store. It had no furniture and most of the dirt floor was hidden under a big pile of rice. Mary and Abby looked at Ann with dismay, but she gave them a faltering smile. "It has a roof and a window! Better than a tent, right?" They unrolled their sleeping mat and fell into exhausted slumber, with Moung Ing curled up under the window outside.

They had no idea this would be their home for the next six months.

In prison, Adoniram began to regain some strength. But exposed to disease and weakened by strain, Ann became ill and could no longer nurse Maria. Little Mary found a woman in the village who provided milk. Moung Ing cooked and bought supplies and delivered messages to Adoniram and watched over them all.

And then the tide of the war changed. British soldiers marched toward Ava and demanded that the Burmese government negotiate with them or be attacked. The king needed interpreters. And that's how Adoniram and Dr. Price finally got released.

The king sent guards to escort the family back to Ava. On their second day back, Adoniram was shipped to the city of Maloun to help negotiate a peace treaty. While he was gone, the kind old governor insisted on caring for Ann and her children at his house.

The British commander declared his terms. In exchange for his withdrawal, he wanted a big pile of money to pay his soldiers, and every foreigner released from Oung-pen-la. The king agreed.

Adoniram's language skills had averted an attack on Ava and won the freedom of his friends. The king offered Adoniram and Dr. Price jobs as court advisors. They decided that wasn't such a good idea, and prepared to leave the region instead.

For the first time in almost two years, the Judson family was finally together.

The governor's servants helped them pack up their house and load everything onto the boats the king had provided. The governor himself came down to the river the night they were to set sail.

"I am so sorry we met under such terrible conditions," he said, rocking nervously on his heels. "Mr. Judson, I hope you can understand that I never wanted you to be locked in my prison. I was only doing my job, and——."

Adoniram stuck out his hand. His grip was not as strong as before, but he was glad his feet had healed enough to walk short distances again. "I hear that you are responsible for saving my life. And I can never thank you for caring so dearly for my Ann."

The governor broke into a smile and pumped his former prisoner's hand. "Oh, yes, of course. Is there anything else you need for your journey? More rice? Oil?"

"You have already given us more than we have room for," said Ann, taking his arm and squeezing it. "Now, you'll read the Scripture papers I left for you, won't you?"

"Yes, yes."

She looked into his dark eyes. "Thank you, my friend, for everything. I pray the rest of your days in Ava will be more peaceful."

Adoniram carried her onto the riverboat. The girls sat down beside her, with Maria tucked into Mary's arms. Adoniram took one last look at the little house on stilts where he had started and abruptly ended this mission effort. Illuminated by a milky half-moon and powered by the river breeze, the Judsons watched from the back of their boat as Ava faded into the waters of the Irawaddy.

Dr. Price later returned to Ava to serve as a counselor to the king and continue his medical mission.

Adoniram, Ann, and Maria had a short reunion. Only a few months after they left, in 1826, Ann's poor health finally gave out. Baby Maria died soon after. Adoniram went into deep depression, helped only by his work translating the Old Testament. But he remained committed to his missionary call. He would marry twice more. Sarah Boardman, a veteran missionary and translator in Burma, became his mission partner and bore him eight children before her death in 1845. Then, during a brief furlough to America, he met and married writer Emily Chubbock, who returned with him to Burma. His own health broken by his twenty-one months of torture, he was ill much of his later years and died at sea in 1850.

FIDELIA FISKE:
GIVE ME YOUR DAUGHTERS

WINTER 1840. SHELBURNE, MASSACHUSETTS.

THROUGH THE WINDOW, she saw the flames leap as her mother tossed the pile of sheets onto the fire. It was the last of the sickbed linens, and they had to be burned in case any of the Typhoid Fever germs remained. The blaze was the only spot of color she could make out against the snowbank.

Fidelia drew the blankets back up to her chin. She heard the doctor's footsteps move away from her room and through the kitchen, and then the squeak of the back door. Turning her face to the window again, she watched as he went out toward the fire with his bag of instruments in one hand. Her mother must have been crying, because he handed her a handkerchief. They spoke for a few minutes, heads bent, before he left around the side of the house. The jingle of sleigh bells confirmed he was off to see his next patient.

A few minutes later, Mrs. Fiske came into her room with a cup of hot water. "How is your headache now?"

"Tolerable," said Fidelia. "Much better than yesterday."

The young woman did not look well. Her eyes were half closed, her lips colorless. But compared to previous days when her skin was flushed and spotted with fever and she thrashed around the bed in pain, she looked far better now, even in her weakened state.

"I'm glad to hear that," her mother said. "The doctor is confident you will make a full recovery."

"Yes, the fever seems to have passed. He said I might expect headaches and stomach aches for awhile, but by spring perhaps I'll be much stronger."

Mrs. Fiske held the cup to her daughter's lips and helped her drink. Then she sat down in the small cane chair, the only piece of furniture in the room besides the bed and a tall linen chest. Fidelia could see that she had scrubbed the tears from her face, but her eyes were still red from crying.

"God has been merciful to me," Fidelia said quietly.

"Yes, he has," her mother agreed, looking down at her lap. "Nine of your classmates have been taken by the fever. These last few months have been a time of great mourning for many of us."

"I only wish—."

"I know." Her mother reached out and put a hand on her daughter's face. "But your father and your sister wanted nothing more than to care for you in your time of need. They knew they could catch the fever, but they refused to let that keep them from you."

"The Lord gives and the Lord takes away." Fidelia was silent for a moment. "But you, mother! The Lord has spared you, too. You have been so strong in all of this."

"Someone must carry on raising and educating your sisters. And the church work. I'm afraid I have neglected my duties, though the Reverend has been very kind."

"What happens now?"

Her mother stood up. "What happens now is that you must devote yourself to recovery. That is all you need to worry about."

Fidelia reached for her mother's hand. "When I am well, I want to return to Mount Holyoke for my last year."

"I know you do. And you shall, provided you recover your strength."

"If I had not been ill, I would be graduating this spring. I could have been teaching by autumn."

"It is only a year's delay. I'm sure you will still finish strong at seminary, Fidelia. I have never doubted your gift for learning." A brief smile crossed her face. "I remember you sitting near the fireplace with Cotton Mather's and Timothy Dwight's books spread across your eight-year-old knees. Few adults can boast they have read them, but you did it when you were a child!"

"They were father's favorite books," Fidelia remembered.

"And now they are your books," her mother said, tucking the blanket under the young woman's chin. "You can take them with you when you go back to Mount Holyoke. But first, you must rest."

"Yes, mother—and thank you."

"Sleep," said her mother, and shut the door.

The winter was long and Fidelia spent all of it in bed, slowly regaining her strength. Her sisters and friends from her church came in to sit with her and relate all the Shelburne local news. She read part of each day until the headaches forced her to rest. She wrote letters of sympathy to the families of her classmates who had died. And she spent a lot of time thinking about why she was spared.

Spring came. The earth thawed and became green again. On warmer days, Fidelia wrapped herself in a shawl and went out to her rocking chair on the lawn. Those naps in a patch of yellow sunlight were good for her body and her soul.

She passed the summer reading and preparing to return to school. Most days she was well enough to go for a long walk, and she sometimes went as far as the small churchyard. There she would rest in front of the two mounds of dirt that marked the graves of her father and sister.

By August, the doctor agreed she was well enough to go back to school. "Just don't push yourself too hard," he warned, "or you will weaken again. Keep getting plenty of rest."

A few weeks later, her mother kissed her goodbye and put her in a stagecoach to South Hadley. "Remember the doctor's orders!" she urged, waving on the other side of the coach window.

As they pulled into the drive of Mount Holyoke Female Seminary, Fidelia's heart thrilled at the sight of her beloved school. Two other students had just arrived and were carrying parcels across the lawn. Behind them rose the four-story brick building topped with a row of chimneys.

With the stage driver behind her with her bags, she stepped into the familiar main hall. After the deaths of so many students, she almost expected the library room and the assembly hall to be missing—but there they were, right as she had left them. She went straight to Miss Lyon's apartment on the first floor and knocked.

When Miss Lyon answered the door, her deep-set eyes lit up and a broad smile crossed her face. She was older than Fidelia by twenty years, and the loss of her mother and the students in the Typhoid outbreak had brought out some gray in her charcoal hair.

"Fidelia, my dear!" she cried. "We have so missed you here." She called over two young women who had just exited the library. "Miss Brigham, Miss Waverly, this is Miss Fiske. She will be joining your chore circle while she finishes her final year. Take her bags up to her room, will you please?"

"Yes, Miss Lyon," they said, each grabbing a bag.

"Thank you," said Fidelia. "It is a pleasure to meet you both."

The headmistress put an arm around Fidelia and guided her toward the stairs. "I'm sure you are hungry, and you are just in time for lunch. I have left a daily schedule in your room. Do remember how things work around here?"

"Yes, Miss Lyon."

"You will have a lot of memorization to do for your classes, but I'm sure that won't be a problem for you."

"No, Miss Lyon."

"You will also need to keep up on your domestic work," she called back as she led the way up to the third floor. "I will introduce you to the other women in your circle later. This month they are responsible for sorting and delivering mail. Do not be late for your meals. Do not miss chapel services. And above all, stay up on your reading."

"Reading is my favorite part," Fidelia assured her.

"I know, and I'm glad. Too many students complain about the reading."

They stopped outside the door of Fidelia's room. Miss Lyon leaned in and lowered her voice. "We're going to be adding to our faculty next year. If you do well this semester, I plan to recommend you for a position."

"Oh, thank you! I won't disappoint you."

"Very well." She smiled again. "It is so good to have you back. I keep praising God for sparing your life and mine."

Fidelia was soon back in the routine of college. First thing each morning, she opened her Bible for devotions. Then it was down to the dining room for breakfast and outside for a brisk one-hour walk with her fellow students. After chapel in the assembly hall, she went to the library to write compositions and memorize texts to be recited. Lunch was followed by lectures and study groups and chores with her circle. She often went back to the library after dinner to stay on top of her long reading list. Evening devotions in her room was the last activity before lights out.

There were days when she feared she was still too weak to keep up with such a demanding schedule. But she was mindful of the doctor's words, and Miss Lyon occasionally let her skip her chores to rest or go to bed early.

The school year quickly passed, and Fidelia graduated with a great sigh of relief. And then a second happy occasion arrived when the seminary's trustees voted to hire her as a teacher for the next year. Mrs. Fiske was pleased. Not only had her daughter survived a deathly illness, but she had also finished a college degree and earned herself a paying job. There was nothing Fidelia was more gifted for than teaching, her mother believed.

For a time, Fidelia agreed with her. And she loved teaching! But as her first semester as a professor got underway, she found her heart drifting. But she wasn't ready to say anything about it yet.

One evening, Fidelia was in the library with a fellow teacher, preparing for the next day's lectures. Combing the shelves of books, she saw a volume labeled "Eight Years' Residence in Persia," written by a Reverend Justin Perkins. "Look," she said to her friend. "A book about the land of Queen Esther."

The two women sat down together and flipped through the pages. It was full of stories about the people of Persia, the culture, the languages, the religions, and the great spiritual and physical needs. The pages were adorned with colorful illustrations.

"Their clothes are beautiful," said Fidelia's friend, running her fingertips over the page.

"They are," Fidelia agreed.

But the next page had a picture of a group of poor children. "How sad!" said the other teacher. "Reverend Perkins says there are thousands of homeless children."

"Most of them are little girls," Fidelia read with dismay, "abandoned on the streets because their fathers can only afford to feed the sons. Or they are married off while still children or sold into slavery!" Fidelia looked away for a few minutes, and then said casually, "You know, I have thought about being a missionary since I was a little girl."

"Really?"

She nodded. "When I was three, my Uncle Pliny left for missions work in Jerusalem, and I always read his letters with great interest. Then, once, my father's friend Reverend King came to visit. He was a missionary to Greece and he said he wished I could go with him since I asked him so many questions about it."

"Well, why haven't you gone to the mission field then?"

"My mother says my skills are in teaching."

"Clearly they are. But surely other lands are in need of teachers, too?"

Fidelia turned the page again and looked down. The image of a young girl and her mother popped out on the page. "Can you imagine what it would be like to teach little girls like this? To spend your days going out into the streets and finding needy children, caring for them, and teaching them?"

"I suppose if we cannot go to these children ourselves, at least we can lovingly care for those that do," her friend said, and went back to her class preparations.

But Fidelia read on eagerly.

And she wondered what God was telling her when, a few weeks later, Miss Lyon made a special announcement at evening prayers. "As you all know," Miss Lyon said from her place at the front of the assembly hall. "I founded this school to give women an education equal to that of the men's schools, so that as graduates of fine academic distinction and high moral character you will become leaders in our world."

She met the gaze of the students in the front rows. "For some of you that work will take place on the mission field. So I have decided that Mount Holyoke will renew its commitment to foreign missions."

Fidelia straightened up in her chair. She could feel the curiosity ripple through the students and teachers in the hall.

"What does this mean?" Miss Lyon continued. "It means more visiting missionaries will be calling on us here to tell us of their work. It means some of you may be moved to leave here when the time comes and take up another work. I hate to see any of you go far away. But that is, after all, our purpose here, and it is a sacrifice we must be willing to make for each other."

The headmistress paused to let her words sink in. "I ask you to seek God in prayer to make his will known to you as various opportunities are presented in the coming days. And I urge you to accept whatever call he gives you. Go where no one else will go, do what no one else will do."

Fidelia felt both weak and excited as she prepared for bed that night. Miss Lyon's talk seemed to confirm her recent wonderings, and yet she worried that she was not strong enough for such a task. Before she rose from her prayers, she asked God to make it clear if he was leading her away from Mount Holyoke.

One night in January, Miss Lyon made another announcement at the evening prayer meeting. "I have received a message from Reverend Justin Perkins, a missionary in Persia."

Fidelia was startled. Reverend Perkins was the author of the book she'd read over and over!

"Reverend Perkins has a severe need for a teacher. It seems a linguist named Judith Grant built a girls' school in Oroomiah, Persia, which had been a great ministry to the people of that city. But she died several years ago, and they have not found a suitable replacement to carry on her work. I have arranged to meet Reverend Perkins here in one hour. You have that much time to decide if you want to be considered for this position. If you do, you will write me a letter stating why, and drop it into the locked box outside the assembly hall. If you are selected, I will call you to my office."

She nodded across her podium. "Good night, ladies. That is all."

At 7:00, Reverend Perkins arrived at Mount Holyoke and was shown into Miss Lyon's office. She rose quickly to greet him. "Good evening, Reverend. How are Mrs. Perkins and your daughter?"

"They are well, thank you," he said. "My daughter is looking forward to returning to Persia."

She offered him her coat rack and he hung up his winter outerwear. The removal of his heavy muffler and cap revealed long sideburns and a kind forehead just beginning to win out over hair.

"If you will come with me, Reverend, we'll find out if we can help your mission today." She led him out the door and down the corridor, explaining her method of finding out who might be interested.

They stopped near the door of the assembly hall, where a wooden box with a drop slot was attached to the wall. She unlocked the box and the lid popped open.

"Oh my!" she exclaimed.

The box was stuffed with paper. She fished out all the slips and needed Reverend Perkins's help to put them in a stack.

"It appears they were interested," he said, impressed. "There must be 40 letters here!"

They carried them back to her office, and over the next hour read and discussed each one. Some were detailed, highlighting all the reasons the person thought she should be chosen. But one was so brief it got Reverend Perkins's attention.

"Look at this one," he said to Miss Lyon. "It simply says, 'If counted worthy, I should be willing to go.'"

She took the paper he passed to her. "Ah," she said, "this was written by Miss Fiske, one of our instructors."

"She is the only one who has even raised the question of her worthiness. That tells me something about her character."

"Miss Fiske was my best student. She is steady and faithful, and always meets her responsibilities with a positive attitude." She met his gaze. "If she were to join your mission, I would lose one of my most valuable instructors."

"So the question is whether Miss Fiske is more valuable to the work of the kingdom here or on the mission field," he said.

They talked about it for a few minutes, then decided it was up to Fidelia to choose. They decided to offer her the position, and sent for her in her room.

Fidelia was clasping her hands with excitement when she came into Miss Lyon's office. "I—I would most love to go," she stammered when they told her. "I have read your book many times, Reverend Perkins, and since the first I've wondered if I was meant to serve there."

He studied her. "Do you understand the work?"

She thought for a moment and answered carefully. "I cannot claim to understand what I have not yet experienced. But I have learned a lot about Persia from your book. I have been a student and a teacher, so I know the duties of both. And during my recent illness I learned what sick and desperate people need from their caregivers."

"All helpful qualifications," he agreed. He gave her a warm smile. "Miss Fiske, we would be grateful for you to join our labors in Persia."

"Thank you, sir." She glanced at her former teacher. "There is just one thing I need to do first before I can give you my assent."

Fidelia stayed up late that night writing a letter to her mother. She praised her for raising her in Christian truth and service, and then posed her query.

Mother, I hesitate to ask you this question, but why should I? Why fear to ask a Christian mother to do what she perhaps loves to do? The question is this: Are you willing for me to leave you for a foreign land and spend my days pointing others to Christ? The opportunity to be a teacher in Persia has been proposed to me. So I put it to you, and trust heaven will guide your advice. My sisters also have a right to express their feelings. I anxiously await your reply.

Your affectionate daughter, Fidelia

The letter had only thirty miles to go, but the New England

snows were living up to their reputation. It was several days before she received a packet from home, and the contents were disappointing.

Fidelia passed the letters to Miss Lyon.

"Hmm." The headmistress thumbed through the letters, reading quickly. "All of your family members have expressed great concern for your health. They think you might not physically endure such a rigorous journey and the hardships of missionary life." She looked at Fidelia with empathy in her wide eyes. "I'm sorry. I know you would have put your whole heart into the mission work."

Her head hanging low, Fidelia nodded. "I guess I have no choice but to stay. I cannot go in good conscience."

Miss Lyon handed back the envelope. "Reverend Perkins needs a decision immediately so the teacher can return with his family. If it will not be you, then I need to go talk to the other woman we considered."

"I understand," said Fidelia, rising. "I will trust God to give me peace."

The second candidate was asked that night. Fidelia lay in her bed, staring at the shadows on the ceiling. She couldn't sleep, so she finally got up and went down to the library, where she looked through Reverend Perkins's book again. When she got back to her bed, she prayed again for guidance. Had she made a mistake? Perhaps she just needed to wait for the joy to come in God's timing.

A few days later, following chapel, Miss Lyon waved for her to join her. Fidelia made her way past the rows of chairs and met the headmistress at the door of the assembly hall.

"What is it, Miss Lyon?"

"Come to my office, my dear."

When she entered the room, she was surprised to see Reverend Perkins waiting there. He rose to greet them.

"Go ahead, Reverend," said Miss Lyon when they were all seated.

"No point in beating around the bush," he said. "Miss Fiske, we would like you to reconsider joining our work in Persia."

Fidelia tilted her head in confusion. "But what about your other candidate?"

"It seems she has received the same advice from her family as you did, so she has declined to serve."

Miss Lyon leaned across her armchair and put a hand on Fidelia's shoulder. "We know there is still the issue of your mother's displeasure with the idea. But I have to tell you I believe this is your work to do, Fidelia. Your gifts fit the needs. Will you think it over again tonight?"

"And we are, unfortunately, quite pressed for time," added Reverend Perkins. "I have been struggling to keep the school open, but if I cannot find the right teacher soon, I may have no option but to close it."

"Then I will reconsider and give you my answer in the morning."

It was another sleepless night for Fidelia. Before breakfast the next morning, she was knocking at the door of Miss Lyon's apartment.

"I will go," she said as soon as the door opened. "But I don't know how to convince my mother."

The headmistress pursed her lips in thought and then said, "We will go do it together. Meet me out front in an hour."

Fidelia ate breakfast quickly and put on as many layers of clothes as she had. When she stepped out the front door, a sleigh was waiting with one of the students, who was a skillful driver. The road was invisible under heavy snow, and the wind was flinging icy crystals into her face. She secured her hood.

Miss Lyon was right behind her. "Let's go," she said. "Neither of us should be out in the weather any longer than necessary."

They helped each other into the sleigh. With a tug at the reigns and a loud "ya!" the driver maneuvered the horses toward the road. The two teachers burrowed under a pile of furs and watched the ice-covered trees pass by as they flew over the snowdrifts toward Shelburne.

It was well after dark when they arrived at Mrs. Fiske's door. Fidelia's knock roused the family out of bed. They stumbled out to the porch in their nightdresses carrying oil lamps.

"Fidelia!" exclaimed her mother. "Oh my, what has happened? What are you doing here?" But then she recognized the second passenger emerging from her wrappings. "Oh, Miss Lyon, hello! Please, all of you, come in out of this frightful cold."

They tramped into the kitchen. Mrs. Fiske stoked the embers in the stove, and Fidelia's sisters spread out the three travelers' wet woolens to dry. They were soon gathered around the table with a steaming pot of tea.

Fidelia's mother got right to the point. "I don't assume you've come thirty miles just for my tea. This is about Persia, isn't it?"

Miss Lyon nodded respectfully. "Yes, Mrs. Fiske. Fidelia took your previous admonishments to heart and was willing to let another go in her place. But the other woman is no longer available. Reverend Perkins is simply out of time, and we all believe Fidelia is gifted and ready to serve."

"Fidelia in Persia?" her sisters jumped in, all talking at once. "But that is crazy! Look how frail she is. And with no husband to accompany her?"

The room fell silent as everyone turned to Fidelia. She looked at Mrs. Fiske on one side of her and Miss Lyon on the other, and couldn't help noticing that she was sitting between her birth mother and her spiritual mother.

She cleared her throat. "My status as an unmarried woman is, surely, something God honors since his providence has arranged it. As to the issue of my health, I am as well as I will ever be and have learned to care for myself. Despite what you see as shortcomings, I am convinced God wants me to do this. Let me explain how I have come to this decision."

For the next several hours, the Fiske kitchen was lit up with conversation and the glow of the stove. Fidelia told them about the influence of missionaries in her youth, about Reverend Perkins's book about Persia, about the necessary skills she had been gaining, about her daily prayers for guidance. Tears flowed around the table as freely as the tea. Finally, Mrs. Fiske said she needed to sleep on the decision. She found everyone a place to sleep, and the household settled into restless slumber.

The next morning was Sunday, and Fidelia and her guests joined her family in worship at the Shelburne church. Late that afternoon, after they had returned to the house and eaten together, Fidelia's mother asked her to help her with the dishes while the others went upstairs to rest.

"It breaks my heart to do this," her mother said, wiping her wet hands on her apron, "because I know I may never see you again. But I cannot keep you from the Lord's work." She pulled her daughter into her arms. "Go, my child, go. But promise me you will take care of your health."

Fidelia buried her face in her mother's neck and held on. "I will, mother. I promise. Thank you for understanding why I must go."

Her mother pulled away and dabbed at her eyes with her apron hem. "Your father would be proud, my dear. Foreign missions were always close to his heart. We entertained so many missionaries in this kitchen over the years."

"Then I will carry his missionary heart with me. I have to leave in less than two months, so I could use your planning skills."

Mrs. Fiske took off her apron and sat down. "Then let's figure out what needs to be done."

The next morning, Miss Lyon returned to South Hadley in the sleigh. Fidelia stayed behind to make the most of her last days with her family. Her church even threw her a farewell party. By the time she boarded a carriage with many packages from her mother, they were all getting used to the idea that Fidelia was going where

God wanted her to be. But as the carriage pulled away and Fidelia looked back for the last time on her family home, she had to force herself to think about the future so she wouldn't break down.

She finished her preparations at Mount Holyoke, where Miss Lyon had put some of the students to work cutting and stitching a new wardrobe for their missionary. The local pastor came by to deliver medical supplies from his church. She packed up her books and other teaching materials she would need, many supplied by her fellow teachers. Everyone was participating in her send off.

When the carriage came to drive her to Boston where she would board a ship, Miss Lyon stood with her, with most of the school waiting on the lawn. The headmistress was uncharacteristically affectionate, squeezing Fidelia's hand. "Are you sure you have everything?" she said again.

"Yes, Miss Lyon. The way you manage this place, I am quite sure I won't be missing one item!" She smiled. "I owe you so much—my education, my first job, and now this amazing opportunity. How can I thank you?"

"Dear Fidelia, your friendship is reward enough. And you are going into a new world with the light of God. It is precisely for this that I have poured my life into this school."

She threw her arms around her former teacher. "I promise I will write regularly."

"Yes you will, or I will contact Reverend Perkins and have you recalled!"

They laughed, and Fidelia climbed into the carriage. "We will remember you at evening prayers!" Miss Lyon called through the window.

Fidelia put her hand on the glass and watched the school grow small between her fingers as the horses trotted toward the road. "When all life's work is done, we will meet again," she murmured, and let her tears run freely.

By June, Fidelia Fiske, small town New England girl, had

arrived in a big city on the other side of the world. From the port, they traveled hundreds of miles through the mountain passes in a caravan of twenty horses. To avoid the intense heat, they started every morning at 1:00 and rode for eight hours, resting over midday. The Perkins family had a lot of friends along the way, so every week or so, they stopped at someone's home to visit and refresh themselves. Now they were on the final leg of their journey, the village just visible as they crossed over the last rise.

"Oroomiah is a little different from Shelburne and Mount Holyoke, eh?" Reverend Perkins shouted to Fidelia from atop his horse. "And look who is coming out to meet us!" He leaned in the saddle so his little daughter, riding behind him, could see the dark horses approaching in a cloud of dust. The child had become close with the new teacher during their long sea voyage.

Fidelia was wearing a long head scarf for protection against the sun. She brushed it out of her eyes and squinted ahead. "Who are they?" she shouted back.

"Friends!" the little girl cried, clapping her hands with delight.

They came to a stop, and the approaching riders sprang off their horses while they were still in motion. Four young men in loose robes, clean shaven and wearing scarves wrapped around their dark heads, ran to them joyfully. "Welcome back!" one shouted, and gave the Reverend a hearty embrace.

Fidelia dismounted and straightened her skirt.

"Miss Fiske, this is Joseph, the bishop's brother," Reverend Perkins said. "He is a priceless member of our team."

"Hello," she said.

"And this is Abraham, and over here Moses and John, two of our students."

"Glad to see you! Glad to see you!" the men kept repeating.

"Come," said Joseph, urging them to follow him. "The people are waiting."

They got back on their horses and crossed the remaining

distance quickly. Rounded shapes that might have been boulders or grazing flocks grew larger as they approached the edge of town, and Fidelia realized they were people. Lots of people! It looked like the whole village had turned out to meet them.

Reverend Perkins moved his horse in close to hers, and pointed through the dusty haze to a cluster of buildings near the center of the village. "That is where we are going. What do you think of the city so far?"

She wiped the sand and perspiration from her forehead with her sleeve. "I am quite breathless, Reverend! It is an amazing sight. Even your wonderful book does not do justice to it."

They had slowed their horses to a walk. All around them people closed in to shout greetings. She could not follow their language, though she thought it beautiful. The men shouted and smiled. She couldn't tell if the women were smiling because they wore veils, but they were waving. Some of the population looked well-fed, but many were little girls in tattered robes with dirty faces.

"These are your children," he said to her, "the ones their society has deemed worthless because of their gender or illness. You will never run out of students for your Persian Mount Holyoke!"

Now that she could look directly into the girls' eyes, Fidelia's heart ached more than ever to help them. "I need to learn Syriac as soon as possible."

"I can teach you right now the most important phrase you'll say here."

"Please!"

He uttered the foreign syllables, and she tried to repeat them. "What does it mean?" she wanted to know.

He turned and looked her in the eye. "It means, 'Give me your daughters.'"

She gazed around her at the moving mass of people. "Give me your daughters," she said under her breath, "and I will teach them

173

to love God and improve their world." And she urged her horse into the city.

Fidelia Fiske spent 15 years in Persia (modern-day Iran) declaring the value of women. She convinced families to let her educate their young daughters instead of abandoning them or selling them into slavery. She was mother, teacher, and nurse to her students. While maintaining some local cultural expressions like clothing, she developed a curriculum similar to that of Mount Holyoke, training her girls to be messengers of the gospel instead of society's outcasts.

When sickness eventually forced her to return to America in 1858, she toured New England, telling her story to raise interest in foreign missions. She also returned to teaching at Mount Holyoke and published several books, including one on Persian women, one about Mount Holyoke, and a biography of Mary Lyon. She died in 1864.

THE RISE OF PROTESTANT DENOMINATIONS

A DENOMINATION IS an autonomous Christian body, a group of Christians whose beliefs make them distinctive from other Christian bodies. Unlike the historical parish system, in which a person went to a church based on where he or she lived, this system is based on shared values and beliefs. Differences between denominations may be small and few, or they may be great and many. Denominations tend to flourish in places where religious freedom is a serious priority, as in the case of the United States, but they also exist in more closed countries as well.

THE PROTESTANT REFORMATION

Where did denominations come from? Monastic orders and sects have always existed within the church. But the Protestant Reformation in the sixteenth century brought about something different. Soon after Martin Luther posted his "Ninety-Five Theses" in 1517, many teachings differing from Roman Catholicism appeared on the scene. The Protestant Reformation was well underway, yet without an organizing body to keep all Protestants together.

Many people identified with the Reformation but they did not live in the same place or agree on every detail of doctrine. Those who appealed to Luther's teachings called themselves Lutherans, and those who followed Calvin called themselves Reformed. Others thought that Luther and Calvin did not go far enough on certain issues like baptism; they were called Anabaptists. In order to unite Christians, theologians wrote *confessions of faith*. These spelled out particular teachings upon which many could agree. For example, Lutherans wrote the Augsburg Confession, which helped to unite them as heirs of Luther.

HOW DENOMINATIONS ARE FORMED

But confessions do not make a denomination, and many factors can contribute to the formation of a new denomination.

Some denominations hold to the same confession, but remain divided for geographical and political reasons. When the American Revolution occurred, for example, the Church of England as the state church was no longer welcomed in the colonies. Congregations in America that were formerly a part of the Church of England formed the Protestant Episcopal Church (now the Episcopal Church in the United States of America). Methodists who were also a part of the Church of England during the American Revolution eventually organized the Methodist Episcopal Church.

Prior to the American Revolution, churches were primarily either Congregational (especially in New England), Presbyterian, or Anglican. Other groups existed but did not have the presence and strength of these three. After the war, political independence encouraged religious independence. Americans saw a greater number of Baptists, Methodists, and Roman Catholics.

Similarly, as Lutheran immigrants entered North America, they formed new churches and some of those churches joined to form *synods*. This left several distinct synods in America which, though they had separate governments, were theologically united. (In the early twentieth century, many of these would merge to form a single denomination—a practice Lutherans would continue throughout the century.)

Sometimes denominations split over theological disagreements. For example, in 1843, members of the Church of Scotland separated over issues related to the Westminster Confession of Faith, and formed the Free Church of Scotland. And in America, the Presbyterian church split for a short time over the issue of the First Great Awakening. Some (Old Side) were against the Awakening because they thought it was emotionally excessive. Others (New Side) promoted these revivals as a movement of the Holy Spirit. The split lasted from 1741 to 1758, when they reunited.

Many churches that split do not reunite later. Some of these congregations split again and again down the road, unable to come to agreements. Others, however, intentionally look for other Christians they can work with, and sometimes even unite with other denominations to which they had not been connected before.

And some congregations form independently, without the assistance of an established denomination, and do not want to be identified with a denomination. These sometimes form a loose fellowship with other independent churches for the sake of mutual encouragement, without giving up their independence.

A FUTURE WITHOUT DENOMINATIONS

Many Christians long for the day when there will be no more denominations and no more disagreements among the followers of Jesus. They live and worship according to their convictions, but look forward to the event described in Revelation 7:9 (NIV):

"After this I looked and there before me was a great multitude that no one could count, from every nation, tribe, people and language, standing before the throne and in front of the Lamb. They were wearing white robes and were holding palm branches in their hands. And they cried out in a loud voice: 'Salvation belongs to our God, who sits on the throne, and to the Lamb.'"

S⊕JΘURNER TRUTH AND HARRIET
BEECHER STΘWE: IS GΘD DEAD?

AUTUMN 1853. ANDOVER, MASSACHUSETTS.

THE NEW ENGLAND evening was early and
only just beginning to cool. Crisp leaves scudded along
the street, swirling around the feet of the old woman
and her grandson. The boy was skipping and kicking
up stones and dust. But the grandmother walked with
shoulders back and a long stride. Past trees with fading
colors, they made their way toward a large wooden
house and stopped before the porch. A potted fern
greeted them from the step.

The sun had not yet set, but the lamps on the second
floor were already lit. The old woman could see that the front
room was full of people passing by the windows. The murmur of
their chatter floated out to the street.

"Come, James," she said, taking the ten-year-old's hand. "We
mustn't waste time just standing here. We didn't come to meet the
house but its owner."

She gave the wide-paneled door a sharp rap with her knuckles.
It was opened immediately by a pale young woman with red hair.

The girl looked up in surprise at the six-foot-tall grandmother with the fierce ebony face.

"Good evening, ma'am. Can I help you?"

At his grandmother's side, the boy bounced on his toes. "We're here to see Mrs. Harriet Beecher Stowe, please," he said.

The girl smiled at his politeness. "And you are?" she asked.

"James Caldwell," the boy announced, arching his chin in the air with pride. "Pleased to meet you."

The servant looked back at the woman. "And you, ma'am?"

"My name is Sojourner Truth. I'm here to meet Mrs. Stowe." Her voice was deep as a man's and had a Dutch accent.

"Mrs. Stowe has a house full of guests this evening, ma'am," said the girl, her hand on the doorknob. "You might call again tomorrow."

The woman shook her head firmly. "I'm here now," she said, pulling her grandson toward the door. The girl glanced at the woman's broad shoulders and large hands and stepped aside as she strode into the house. With a flutter of her apron ties, the girl followed the unexpected visitors inside, past the staircase and into the parlor.

Sojourner Truth stood in the middle of the room and surveyed it top to bottom. The walls were hung with yellow wallpaper and framed oil paintings of birds and plants. A painted screen stood in front of the small fireplace. Above it, a carved shelf rose from the mantel to display an ivory clock.

"I'll wait for Mrs. Stowe here," said Sojourner, and planted herself in an embroidered chair. James moved quickly to stand behind her.

The girl twisted her pale hands in her apron for a moment, unsure how to respond. Then she ducked out of the room. In the parlor, they heard her footsteps clicking up the stairs.

On the second floor, the sitting room was full of people. Several clergymen and their wives had enjoyed dinner with the Stowes.

They were laughing and arguing about politics when the red-haired maid came in and stood close to the mistress of the house.

Harriet Beecher Stowe leaned toward her as the girl announced the extra guests waiting in the parlor. Her arched eyebrows shot up. "Are you quite certain?"

The conversation around her came to a stop as the guests turned toward their hostess.

The girl nodded.

Harriett set her glass on a tray and stood, motioning to her guests to stay seated. "Please, everyone, continue. I'll return in a moment."

She headed toward the stairs, lifting the hem of her skirt as she descended. The talk bubbled up again above her.

As soon as Harriet stepped into the downstairs parlor, Sojourner raised her tall frame from the chair and came forward to meet her. Her long black arms reached out to squeeze the other woman's pale hands. "The author of *Uncle Tom's Cabin*," said Sojourner, receiving Harriet as if she were the guest in Sojourner's home. "The Lord bless you for writing that book."

"Thank you," said Harriet. She had to lift her head to meet her visitor's wide-set eyes.

It was natural that these two famous women, meeting for the first time, looked each other over.

Sojourner noticed the petite woman's dark blue gown, which fastened down the middle with a row of tiny buttons. A hair ribbon held back wispy curls, giving her face an open look. She was clearly surprised by her unexpected guest, but maintained the smile of a gracious hostess.

Under her bonnet, Sojourner's thick hair was white at the temples, fading into black. Creases circled her mouth, but her cheeks were smooth. Harriett could not guess how old she was. And her hands bore the callouses of hard labor though she was dressed as a modest lady.

"James!" Sojourner chided, breaking the silence. "Where are your manners?"

"I'm sorry," said James, coming around from behind the chair and giving Harriet a practiced nod. "Nice to meet you, Mrs. Stowe."

Harriet gave him her hand as she would a gentleman. "Hello, James."

"My grandson," Sojourner explained.

"I see. Shall we sit?" Harriet gestured to the furniture.

Sojourner balanced on the tiny chair again. James went to sit at her feet, but Harriet insisted he help himself to his own seat.

"I reckon you've heard of me?" said Sojourner.

Harriet nodded. "I have, Miss Sojourner. A former slave working to end slavery. I understand you travel the country giving lectures."

"Fact is I just lectured in New York."

"Ah, that is why you came by tonight."

"Yes. I regret interrupting your party. But I could not wait until my next time through Massachusetts to see you. At my age, I have learned not to put things off. I do not know how many years God will use me to stir this nation to repent from their sins against my people."

"Our backgrounds are different, but I believe our message is the same."

"We have the truth in common, Mrs. Stowe."

Harriet hesitated, and then said, "I wonder if I might persuade you to stay awhile. Would you mind if I invite my guests down? I am sure they have heard of you and would be delighted to meet you."

Sparks lit up Sojourner's dark eyes. "I never pass up an opportunity to deliver God's message."

Harriet called for her guests to join them in the parlor. The curious group was quick to file down the stairs and crowd into the small room. James abandoned his seat to make room for the adults and went back to standing behind his grandmother's chair. The ladies settled side-by-side on the sofa while the men clustered in the corner. Their hostess introduced each person by name, and then took the last man by the arm and drew him toward her unusual guest.

"Miss Sojourner, this is my brother, the famous minister, Dr. Henry Ward Beecher."

"An honor, ma'am," he said.

Sojourner took in the gentleman's high forehead, drooping jowls, and hair flowing down to his collar. "You're famous, eh? I love preachers. I'm a preacher myself."

Dr. Beecher blinked at her. "Oh? You preach from the Bible?"

She shook her head. "Can't read a word of it," she said gravely. "Never learned to read. But I have one sermon I preach, the one I call 'When I Found Jesus.'"

"The best kind of sermon!" exclaimed one of the women.

"Indeed," agreed Sojourner.

Harriet sat down again, this time with her brother at her side. "How did you find Jesus, Miss Sojourner? Please tell us your story."

Sojourner's smile disappeared. She stared at the floor for nearly a full minute. Harriet was beginning to think she had offended her guest when the old woman sat up very straight and turned her fierce gaze on the other guests.

"We all heard right away that the State of New York was to free us slaves in 1827. My master, Mr. John Dumont, promised that if I worked hard enough, he would free me before the state law was enforced. But I injured my hand. Figuring that he wouldn't get as much work out of me, he went back on our deal."

Harriet found her visitor's gaze mesmerizing. "What did you do?" she wanted to know.

"I worked twice as hard as before! I began to pray fervently for freedom. But Mr. Dumont refused to recognize my labor. One night, while praying, I felt as if God was telling me it was time to leave on my own."

"You broke the law?" said Henry Beecher, frowning.

"No," the old woman insisted. "I merely made Mr. Dumont stick to his word. I grabbed my daughter, Sophia, one day just before daybreak, and fled over the hills."

"Your daughter?" murmured Harriet. "You had a family?"

"I had several children with my husband Thomas." Sojourner's broad lips tightened. "By law, every child I bore became a slave of my master. He didn't have to free them until they were middle age—if they lived so long. I couldn't bear for Sophia to suffer as I did."

"What about your husband?" asked one of the women.

Sojourner crossed her arms over her chest. "Thomas was content to stay there," was all she would say about it. "But I ran up the hills with my girl. When the sun rose in the morning, I wasn't sure where to go. I went a few miles before I recognized the home of a friend, Mr. Levi Rowe. I hadn't seen Mr. Rowe in a long time. I soon discovered he was on his deathbed, bless his soul. He and his wife told me about the good people Mr. and Mrs. Van Wagener, not far away."

From the corner of her eye, Harriet noticed that James was nodding off, leaning against the back of his grandmother's chair. She waved to the red-headed maid, who was standing in the doorway.

"Yes, Mrs. Stowe?"

"Get some water for Miss Sojourner and her grandson, please."

"Yes, Mrs. Stowe."

"Would you care for something to eat, James?" Harriet asked him.

He perked up. "Yes, ma'am. Thank you, ma'am."

"And bring an apple for the young man."

The girl slipped away. Harriet turned her attention back to Sojourner. "Please continue."

"Well, I wasn't at the Van Wagener home for too long before Mr. Dumont tracked me down. When Mr. Van Wagener opened his door, Mr. Dumont saw me standing there in the room. He smiled and pointed at me. 'There you are,' he said. 'So you've run away.' He'd come to take us back."

"What did you do?" asked Henry. He was leaning forward in his seat.

"I told him I wasn't going nowhere!" Sojourner uncrossed her arms and shook a long forefinger at them. "He said to me, 'Well, I'll take the child then,' and pointed to Sophia. But Mr. Van Wagener, a man who just don't think it is right to own slaves, offered money to my master for the remainder of our year in service. Mr. Dumont took the money and left. I didn't know what to expect, but when I called Mr. Van Wagener 'master,' thinking he gone and bought me, he objected. Mrs. Van Wagener told me that there is only one master and he is the master of us all."

"Amen," said Harriet.

"Indeed!" said Henry.

"I didn't know their master then," Sojourner explained. "I knew there was a God, but I didn't know Jesus. I'd heard of him, but thought he was no more powerful than General Lafayette."

"He's much bigger than Lafayette!" James offered from beside the chair.

Harriet laughed. The maid arrived with a tray of water glasses and fruit. Sojourner thanked her and drained her glass all at once. James sipped at his. Then he kneeled down on the floor, settled his backside on his feet, and began to nibble at the apple.

Sojourner went right on with her story. "One night, I went to a meeting of Methodists. People everywhere at this meeting were singing and praying. Person after person got up to tell us about their past sins and how Jesus changed them. I knew that I believed in this Jesus. I think he'd been leading me all along. A rush of love came into my soul. A rush of love like I'd never known. It was amazing, pure amazing!"

"Not long after, I went to the house of Dumont to visit my family. Mr. Dumont's mistress was home in bed, as she often is. She doesn't much like me. Never did. My son Pete was no longer there. I found out that a man who was borrowing him from the Dumonts sold him to another man who lived in Alabama."

Her deep voice lowered almost to a growl. "In New York, he was to be freed at the age of twenty-one, according to the law. To sell him to someone in another state is illegal!"

Her black eyes flashed, remembering her anger. Harriet and her guests waited respectfully for her to continue.

"Well, I charged up to Mrs. Dumont and demanded my son back. You know what she said to me?"

"What did she say?" asked Henry, on the edge of his seat.

"She looked me up and down and said, 'What a noise you're making over one little slave boy.' I stared her straight in the eyes and told her, 'I'll have my son again, I will.' Then she said, 'Fine. Go get your son, but it's gonna be hard without any money.'"

Sojourner gripped the edges of her shawl with clenched fingers. "Well, I looked at her, remembered all the great things God did for those Methodists at that meeting, and I told her, 'God has plenty of money. He'll get my son back for me.' And I was sure of it, too. Why, I felt so tall within—I felt as if the power of a nation was with me!"

"The power of the Lord is greater even than the power of a nation!" said Henry.

"Miss Sojourner," said Harriet. "That reminds me of another story I recently heard about you."

Everyone turned to Harriet.

"Is it true that when the famous abolitionist Frederick Douglass was speaking in Faneuil Hall in Boston a few years ago, he suggested that it might be time to free the slaves by force? And is it true that you were there, and you stood up and shouted, 'Frederick, is God dead?'"

Sojourner rocked her whole upper body in her chair. "Indeed I did say that, Mrs. Stowe. I was concerned that my brother Mr. Douglass was so upset about the state of things that he had given up on the power of God. But we mustn't ever forget that God is alive and he can do anything! He sure helped me with my son."

Henry Beecher glanced over at James. The drowsy boy was leaning his head against the side of the chair, the apple core about to roll out of his cupped hand. Dr. Beecher whispered, "James!"

The boy's eyes flew open.

"There is a room upstairs," Henry offered. "Would you like to go up and sleep?"

"Maybe we should be moving on," said Sojourner, tucking her shawl around her arms. "We don't want to be a bother."

"Oh no," insisted Harriet. "We all want to hear how you got your son back."

The other guests murmured their agreement.

"In fact," Harriet went on, "unless your travel is urgent, you must be our guests for a few days. I have already written about the plight of the black slaves, but I want to do more. I am very interested in your experiences as an abolitionist. Won't you and James remain with us for another day or two?"

For the first time all evening, Sojourner's face broke out in a wide smile that revealed her false teeth. She always told James that her teeth were the only thing false about her.

"Very kind of you, Mrs. Stowe. I'm glad to know the writer of *Uncle Tom's Cabin* better."

"It's settled then," said Harriet. She called to her maid again and asked her to show James upstairs and prepare the guest room.

Henry turned his attention back to Sojourner. "But before the night is over, please tell us what happened with your son."

"Yes, please continue," urged Harriet.

Sojourner pressed her broad shoulders into the back of the chair again. "First I went to the mother of the man who sold my boy, Mrs. Fowler. But she just mocked me. I didn't know what I could do next, so I prayed to God for help. Then I met a man, who to this day does not want me to say who he was. He told me where to find some friends who could help. They were Quakers, and kind people. They invited me in, gave me lodgings, and listened to my story. Then they told me that in the morning I had to go to the courthouse and make a complaint to the Grand Jury."

She raised her arms in a shrug. "Well, I went to the courthouse the next day like they said. But I didn't know nothing about Grand Juries. I told my story to the first man I saw. But he told me he wasn't the Grand Jury and I should go upstairs. So I went upstairs and asked this finely-dressed man if he was the Grand Jury. He wanted to know what my complaint was. Well, when he heard it he said it was a serious one. So he pointed me to a room. 'There you'll find a Grand Jury,' he said."

"They arranged for me to meet with the people who made up the Grand Jury. It cost me some money, and I didn't have any. But two Christian lawyers and that kind Quaker family gave me what I needed."

"And then you got your son back?" prompted Harriet.

"The man who sold him was threatened with large fines if he didn't return him to me. After months of travel, I finally got my son back. But he didn't recognize me at first. And worse, his back was covered with scars and lumps from where Mr. Fowler flogged him." The old woman gave a deep sigh. "I was glad to have him back though. God knew what he was doing. That man, Fowler, who abused my Pete—why, later on he killed his own sister!"

"Oh my!" Harriet exclaimed.

"Yes. If God was dead, my Pete would've been dead, too. But God was very alive and watching out for my boy."

The room was quiet. Sojourner yawned. All the walking and talking of the day had wearied her. The guests noticed and began to rise from their seats.

"I'm afraid it is time for us to go home, Mrs. Stowe," said one of the men.

"Yes, my dear," said one of the women, taking Harriet's arm. "Thank you for such an interesting and unexpected evening."

Before they left, each guest passed by Sojourner and shook her hand, thanking her for telling her story. They congratulated her on winning her son back and promised to pray for her work.

When the maid had shut the front door behind the last guest, Harriet and Henry walked Sojourner to the foot of the staircase. Henry paused there. "Miss Sojourner, I must ask you one more question tonight."

She was several inches taller than he, and looked down at him patiently. "Yes, preacher?"

"What is the origin of your name?"

"Oh, yes," nodded Harriet, "it is such a curious name. Have you always gone by it?"

Sojourner smiled again, but did not show her teeth. "No. I was named Isabella at birth. Just Isabella. Slaves are not given last names, but use the surname of their master when they need one. But when I left the house of bondage, I left everything behind!" She was gesturing with her fist. "I went to the Lord and asked him for a new name. He calls me by the name Sojourner, because he wants me to travel around this land telling people of their sin. And he calls me Truth, because I'm supposed to tell them the truth."

She pulled out a slip of paper from a large pocket in her dress. In large letters, it read, "Proclaim liberty throughout all the land unto all the inhabitants thereof."

"I journey to camp meetings and tell people about their sins and about Jesus who takes away their sins," she said. "A great number of persons come to hear me preach."

He gave her a formal little bow. "There is more truth in what I've heard tonight than in many a sermon. I hope to see you and James again before you depart," he said, and lifted his hat from the coat rack by the door.

She raised her hand in blessing. "Good night, Dr. Beecher."

"If you will follow me," said Harriet, leading the way upstairs. She showed her into a comfortable bedroom. Little James was already asleep under the quilt, and the maid had left a fresh towel next to the filled wash basin.

"Thank you for your kindness, Mrs. Stowe."

Harriet paused at the door. "I am so glad you stopped by tonight," she said, quietly so she wouldn't wake the boy. "We have much to discuss. You know, at first, I didn't believe I could write a book. But I did want to change the way people think about slavery."

"Getting people to change is always hard. But God has a way of making it happen."

Harriet leaned against the doorframe. "When I moved to Cincinnati, near the Ohio River, I heard so many stories of slaves trying get across the river to find their freedom. Women would carry their infants across the frozen river, hoping to find a new life. But they often died in the process. I realized that slavery is cruel and against the law of God, and I wanted to do something about it. It was my sister-in-law who challenged me to write a novel about it. And so I wrote *Uncle Tom's Cabin*."

"Haven't read a word of it," Sojourner admitted, "but I'm told that it's softened many hearts to my cause. That's why I wanted to see you before I left town. I wanted to thank you."

"You are a remarkable woman! I pray you will keep lecturing, and I will keep writing. Maybe one day we will see the end of slavery."

"I reckon we will," said Sojourner confidently. "Remember, we are not alone in our task. God is not dead!"

"Amen to that!"

Harriet left her then, and Sojourner got ready for a good night's sleep beside her beloved grandson.

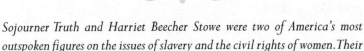

Sojourner Truth and Harriet Beecher Stowe were two of America's most outspoken figures on the issues of slavery and the civil rights of women. Their work led to major reforms in America, and both women were recognized formally by President Abraham Lincoln.

Shortly after she met Sojourner Truth, Harriet Stowe wrote a second novel about slavery called Dred. *In 1863 she wrote, "Sojourner Truth, The Libyan Sibyl," an article about her unexpected meeting with Sojourner. In 1896, Stowe died in Hartford, Connecticut, where she lived next door to another famous American writer, Mark Twain.*

Sojourner, who could not read or write, later dictated her life story in the now famous book, The Narrative of Sojourner Truth. *She never knew the exact date of her birth, but lived well into her eighties. She died in Battle Creek, Michigan in 1883. Her gravestone bears the quote, "Is God Dead?"*

DAVID LIVINGST⊕NE:
I LEAVE IT WITH Y⊕U

DECEMBER 4, 1857. CAMBRIDGE UNIVERSITY, ENGLAND.

THE LECTURE HALL was nearly full. But the long line of professors, students, and politicians continued to elbow into the back rows, their shuffling amplified by the marble floor. Afternoon light streamed in the double rows of windows, casting a warm glow on the carved oak paneling. The elegant Senate House rarely drew such a large crowd.

The weathered man on the platform looked uncomfortable in his black waistcoat and ribbon bowtie. He twisted one end of his drooping mustache and snuck a glance at the audience gathering to hear him speak.

A gentleman at the far edge of the front row nodded in his direction. Politely, he returned the gesture, feeling the familiar twinge in his shoulder as he stretched.

He picked up the book resting on the chair next to him. "Missionary Travels and Researches in South Africa by Dr. David Livingstone," the cover declared. The pages smelled of fresh ink as he turned them. It seemed unreal that his adventures had been recorded in this book. But then, when he thought about it, having those adventures had been much more surprising.

"My shoulder, for example," he thought. "How many Scotsmen have been mauled by a lion?" It had happened years ago, but the recurring pain kept fresh his memory of that day.

He had been working in the African village of Mabotsa, a site he had planned for a missionary station. It was one of those places where the earth seems to stretch on forever until it just fades into the sky, with barely a scrub tree to mark the miles. The locals raised cattle on the sparse patches of grass. But lately there had been trouble. A pride of lions had settled into the area and started attacking the herds.

Mebalwe, the local schoolmaster, asked the missionary to join some of the men on a lion hunt. "When you kill a lion," he said, "the rest of the pride usually moves on to another hunting ground. If we can take one down, they will go away and our cattle and the whole village will be safer."

Livingstone was a good shot with a rifle, and he was trying to befriend the people. Plus, a lion hunt was just too exotic to pass up. So he agreed to go the next day.

After a few hours of searching, the group spotted a large male lion dozing on a boulder. Slowly, they crept through the knee-high clumps of grass and formed a circle, closing in on the beast. Their rifles and spears were poised for battle.

"Shoot, Mebalwe," urged one of the men in a hoarse whisper.

Mebalwe raised his rifle. He aimed. He fired. He missed! Shards of rock scattered, and the lion roared to life. He leaped over the hunters, landing behind them and snarling.

"Don't let him get away!" shouted Livingstone. "Spear him! Spear him!"

But the hunters didn't want to get close enough to the lion to spear him. So they raised their rifles and tried again to surround the animal, now tossing his mane in warning.

Livingstone scrambled into place. But, looking up as he passed a bush, he found himself just thirty yards from a second, bigger lion! Immediately he drew his gun and emptied both barrels.

The lion shrank back in pain, but the shots had not been fatal. He threw his head back and loosed a deafening roar.

Livingstone hoped his companions were taking aim to cover him, but then he heard shouting behind him. He glanced back and saw the others running away from him, still chasing the other lion. "Take him!" they were shouting.

"No, wait!" cried Livingstone.

They looked back and Mebalwe screamed. "Behind you, Dr. Livingstone!"

He turned in time to see the sun eclipsed by the shadow of a lion, the enormous paws bearing down on him. With a shocking crunch, the lion seized Livingstone's shoulder and shook him back and forth. "Like a rat in the mouth of a terrier," he later described it. His hat spun into the air and disappeared in the grass.

Two shots rang out. The lion released him, and he hit the ground with a crash. He felt the wetness of his shirt as the blood spread across his chest. But there was no pain. His left arm was numb. He let his eyes follow the sound of shouting and gun blasts.

Mebalwe was firing at the lion. The beast leaped over Livingstone's motionless body and charged Mebalwe, catching him in the thigh and tossing him over his shoulder.

Another hunter—a man Livingstone had once saved from a charging buffalo—thrust his spear into the lion's chest. The lion swung around, the end of the spear shoving the man backwards. Again, the lion's jaws latched onto a victim.

Livingstone struggled to stand. But before he could make it to his knees, it was all over. The lion's eyes rolled back, his hind legs gave way, and he collapsed to the sand, dead.

The next day, they burned his carcass on a bonfire. The whole village declared it was the largest lion they had ever seen. The three injured men recovered, but Livingstone's left arm bore the scars of eleven huge teeth and never regained its full strength.

"The lion attack was only one of many perils," murmured Livingstone, lost in his thoughts on the lecture platform. He stared at the page in his book that recounted the story, then flipped past it, noting so many other experiences he could talk about today. Severe desert drought and his confrontation with the heathen rain-doctors. Tribal wars. Deadly diseases transmitted by tiny insects. But he had written out his remarks so he would not get carried away.

Dr. Philpott, the professor who had been sitting with him, was now at the podium. "Thank you all for joining us today on this exciting occasion," he said as the room hushed. "Our lecturer this afternoon is a medical doctor, missionary, and explorer, born in Scotland, but—as we all know—famous for his adventures in Africa. Please welcome Dr. David Livingstone!"

The galleries erupted with applause. Livingstone stepped up to the podium, spread his notes in front of him, and put on his spectacles.

"When I went to Africa about seventeen years ago," he began, "I resolved to gain an accurate knowledge of the many native languages. So while I continued there, I generally spoke only in the African languages, with the result that I am no longer very fluent in my own."

The crowd laughed.

"So I hope you will excuse my imperfections. I will endeavor to give you as clear a picture as I can of what Africa is like."

And he spent the next quarter-hour describing the climate, the animals, the insects, the plants, the cultures of the different regions, even the diseases. His love and respect for the continent of Africa was evident. As he spoke, he saw people in the audience taking notes and marking pages in their copies of his book.

"I went to Africa with the purpose of teaching the doctrines of Christianity, and settled with the tribes on the border of the Kalahari Desert. The chief of one of these tribes was named Sechele. During my first Christian service in his region, he asked many questions about the Bible. I told him about God's future judgment of sinners and the only way of redemption. He was moved, and wanted to know why none of my people had ever come to his land to tell him of this."

The room was silent. Everyone was thinking of the many generations of Africans who had never heard the gospel.

Livingstone cleared his throat. "Of course, I explained that we had to sail the ocean and cross the country to him before we could tell him. But I also told him God promised that one day the whole earth will be covered with the knowledge of Christ. The chief pointed to the Kalahari Desert and said, 'Will you ever get beyond that with your gospel? We who are used to the thirst cannot cross that desert. How can you?' I told him I trusted in Christ's promise. And a few years later that chief was the man who enabled me to cross that desert. He himself went with me and preached the gospel to the tribes beyond it."

Heads bobbed in the audience, expressing their approval.

"My medical training was a great aid in my missionary task. Several nights a week my companions and I held Christian worship services and a lecture on a secular topic to aid their farming or toolmaking. Afterwards, I tended the sick, giving them food and medicine. I can tell you that if you show kind attention to the reckless opponents of Christianity on their beds of sickness, they can never become your personal enemies. Here, if anywhere, love opens the door."

He adjusted his spectacles before going on. "My object in going to the country south of the desert was to instruct the natives in Christianity. But circumstances prevented me from living among them more than seven years. Many of the problems were due to the slave trade practiced by the Dutch Boers."

The Boers. As he said the name, the memories came back to him with sudden sharpness.

It was 1852, and he had set off from the desert heading north to find an east-west passage across the continent. Because the trip would be treacherous, he had put his wife and children on a ship back to Scotland to live with his parents. No one was happy about that—especially his wife, Mary, who had grown up in Africa—but he argued that far away and alive was better than nearby and dead.

After spending a few days collecting supplies, he secured a heavy wagon, drawn by ten oxen, and hired servants to assist him. He would remember the early days of that trip as beautiful. How peaceful to sit on a wagon taking your time, soaking in the sun, appreciating the feel of a rare breeze against your skin!

His journal was his constant companion. He sketched plants. He measured the rainfall and the height of the trees. He mapped every river, every valley, every rocky outcropping. He recorded how he spotted a massive herd of migrating gazelles, tossing their elegant horns as they drank from the Orange River.

"Such information will be useful for every future missionary and adventurer," he told himself. "They will have a better idea what to expect and can be more prepared."

Two months into the trip, he stopped at a tiny station called Kuruman, named after a fountain that irrigated the local fields. His father-in-law, Robert Moffat, another Scottish missionary, lived in Kuruman. Livingstone and his team spent a few days with him and then set out again with fresh food and water.

They had not gone far when the wagon lurched forward with a crunch. Livingstone rolled forward and caught himself by bracing his hands against the back of the oxen.

"Woah!" shouted the driver.

They examined the bent axle and splintered wheel.

"This will have to be repaired before we can continue," the driver said.

In a fit of temper, Livingstone kicked the wheel. Another spoke fell off. "Well, that is not going to help, is it?" he chided himself.

Later, he would tell people that this broken wheel saved his life.

They went back to Mr. Moffat's farm and spent two weeks waiting for supplies to repair the wagon. But before they could leave again, Dutch farmers in the region, a group of settlers known as the Boers, had started a war with Livingstone's friend Chief Sechele and the BakWena people. The chief's wife escaped the battle and delivered a letter to Moffat and Livingstone. The letter described how the Boers had destroyed Livingstone's home and carried off many of the BakWena as slaves.

Later, Mebalwe, the BakWena schoolteacher and lion hunter, came to Kuruman and confirmed the details of the attack. "I'm sorry about your home," he told Livingstone, his dark head lowered with grief. "The Boers give the white man a bad reputation."

"Sechele has been gathering weapons for a long time now because he suspected the Boers were going to attack," said Moffat. "I suppose the Boers considered that an act of aggression."

Livingstone threw up his hands. "I helped Sechele get some of those weapons! They're for hunting the lions."

"And the Boers burned your home in revenge," said Moffat. "The Boers see the British missionaries as tools of British expansion. They think our kind are here to take over the land for ourselves."

"Some of our countrymen are," said Livingstone, "but I am not one of them. What will become of the BakWena now?"

Mebalwe looked away. "The Boers sell their captives into slavery."

Livingstone stamped his foot. "This slavery must end! I'll make a protest of this to the British government. They must take action!"

"Yes," said Moffat, "and I'm sure they will, but at the speed of government, you would be better off telling your concerns to the antelope."

Livingstone was too upset to appreciate the joke.

"Be grateful for that broken wheel, son," Moffat said gravely. "You were headed right into the battle, and it sounds like they had it out for you. I doubt you would have made it out alive. God must not be done with you yet."

Later, Livingstone wrote about the battle and their conversation for the benefit of future readers of his journal. He had time to write, because news of the war had sent his hired crew into hiding. It was some months until he found a new team willing to continue.

The scenes from those unpleasant days played through his memory in seconds. He realized he was still standing at the podium, with a sea of faces staring at him inside Cambridge's Senate House. He was a long way from the war with the Boers, and yet his stomach still rose with disgust!

He snapped back to the present and found his place in his notes. "Because of the situation with the Boers," he continued, after clearing his throat, "I resolved to go into the country beyond. I soon found that, for the purpose of commerce, it was necessary to find a path to the sea. Why? Because civilization and Christianity must go on together."

This brought cheers of "hear, hear!" from the audience.

"Let me clarify what I mean," he said. He told them what slavery was doing to the people of Africa and the struggles of other missionaries in the region. He explained that by opening a trade route through the continent, they could make the way for the gospel easier. "You see, I think we made a great mistake when Britain went into India and engaged in commerce but was ashamed to also spread the gospel there."

He was preaching now.

"A new prospect is before us of opening Africa to commerce and the gospel. Providence has been preparing the way. Many of the tribes now speak the same trade language, into which Mr. Moffat has already translated the Bible. The people of Central

Africa, especially, desire to participate in trade. But what they sell are their own countrymen to Dutch and Portuguese slave traders, which of course horrifies the poor Africans—and any Christian Englishman. But if we encourage commerce between them and England, we can fulfill their desire to do business other than slavery, and at the same time shine the light of Christianity in the darkest jungles."

He held up his right arm. "Now I know what you are thinking. The natives are not all excited to hear about Christianity. That's true. But I have seen some of them weep in repentance before God. Missionaries to Africa will face many difficulties, but what easy thing has any value? Jesus left his father's throne to come to earth for us. We should be willing to leave England and go to Africa for him."

There was clapping from some in the audience, as others shifted in their seats. He was calling them to action, and they knew it.

"People say I have sacrificed to do this work. It is true that it has required sacrifice, and I have many regrets." His face grew sober as he thought of his wife and children, whom he had spent so many years away from. That had been difficult on all of them, especially his son. He swallowed hard.

"But it is also a privilege," he went on again. "You have graciously welcomed me back to Britain, and for that I thank you. But I long much more to hear my Lord say, 'Well done, good and faithful servant.'"

He paused and leaned over the podium, giving the audience a hard look. "I beg to direct your attention to Africa. I am going back there to try to make an open path for commerce and Christianity. But I know that in a few years I shall be cut off in that country which is now open. Do not let it be shut again! You must carry out the work which I have begun."

He banged his fist on the podium to drive home his final point. "I leave it with you!" he shouted.

And with that, he snatched up his papers from the podium and threw himself back into the chair behind it.

The crowd rose as one, with whistles and applause.

Afterwards, Dr. Philpott led him to a reception room, where he was soon surrounded by reporters and students with questions. When the crowd thinned, he saw a man waiting patiently to meet him. It was the dark-haired man who had nodded to him from the front row before the lecture.

"Dr. Livingstone," he said, holding out his hand to shake the explorer's. "I am a representative of Charles Mackenzie, a missionary in Africa. We are leading a call to organize the support of Cambridge, Oxford, and other universities for a mission organization based on your work."

"A good effort," agreed Livingstone. "May God bless it."

"I just want to thank you. Your journeys have prepared the way for many missionaries to go to Africa. Without your descriptions of life and the needs there and your discoveries of new routes, we would be entering Africa blind."

"Well, I did not make a lot of converts myself, but I trust that you and your colleagues will use my experience to achieve greater success."

The man seemed encouraged by that and drew himself taller. "Then might I ask for your continued help?"

Livingstone raised his eyebrows. "I am not returning to Africa as a missionary but as an explorer. Some of the members of my missionary society do not see my exploration as missions work and won't support me anymore. But the government is sponsoring an expedition to explore the Zambezi River. So if the government will pay for God's work, then I am willing to do it."

"Oh," the man said, nodding his head rapidly, "but we understand how important your work is. We are ready to pick up the mantle of direct missions work. But we hope you will guide and help us make contacts when we arrive in Central Africa. Will you?"

The creases on Livingstone's face deepened in a broad smile for the first time that day. "Well, I said I was leaving it to you, didn't I? So you let me know when you arrive and I will do whatever I can for you and Dr. Mackenzie."

Dr. Philpott was already leading the explorer away, but the man happily called after him. "Oh, thank you, Dr. Livingstone! Your assistance will be such an encouragement to us all!"

Soon two African expeditions were in the works. Livingstone finished his tour of England and prepared to return to Africa to open up trade routes. And the fledgling missionary society packed their Bibles to start a new mission.

Of David Livingstone's several journeys, his 1852-1856 expedition to look for an east-west passage was his most famous. At the time he delivered this speech, he was one of the most famous people in all of Britain. He took advantage of his fame to argue for the end of the slave trade in Africa. Two years later, he returned to Africa with government support as he planned, but his team found him difficult to work with and this second expedition was less successful than the first. His wife, Mary, joined him again but died soon after her arrival.

Charles Mackenzie led the Universities' Mission to Central Africa, and with Livingstone set up a mission station. But because of their opposition to the slave trade, they were slow to build support in the region.

In his last venture, Livingstone set out in 1866 to find the source of the Nile River. When reports of his death began to circulate, a newspaper reporter spent a year searching for him. Henry Morton Stanley found Livingstone in Ujiji on October 23, 1871. His famous account of the event claimed his first words to the missing explorer were, "Dr. Livingstone, I presume?" Stanley joined his excursion for two more years, until Livingstone died on May 1, 1873. His body was returned to England, where his journals were published as The Last Journals of David Livingstone.

⊕THER CHRISTIANS ⊕F THE AWAKENING CHURCH

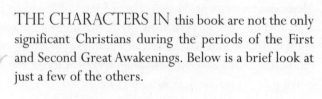

THE CHARACTERS IN this book are not the only significant Christians during the periods of the First and Second Great Awakenings. Below is a brief look at just a few of the others.

William Tennent (1643-1746) was born in Scotland and graduated from the University of Edinburgh. He moved to America after living in Ireland and joined the Presbyterian church. He was a revivalist leader who trained revival ministers in his home in Neshaminy, Pennsylvania, which became known as the Log College. His school met with controversy when he invited the Methodist revivalist George Whitefield to preach there.

Gilbert Tennent (1703-1764) was the son of William Tennent. A Presbyterian clergyman born in Ireland, he spent most of his life in America, where he graduated from the Log College and Yale. One of the leaders of the Great Awakening,

Tennent emphasized the need for a person to know if he or she is converted. He worried that those ministers who opposed the Great Awakening were not truly Christian. When in his famous sermon, "The Danger of an Unconverted Ministry," he accused Presbyterian ministers of being unregenerate, he started a schism in the church. After the First Great Awakening, he led a successful effort to reunite Presbyterians. When the Log College closed in the 1740s, Gilbert, along with three other Log College graduates and other pro-revivalists, helped to start The College of New Jersey, an Evangelical school that was later renamed Princeton University.

George Whitefield (1714-1770) was a popular Evangelical revival preacher during the First Great Awakening. While at Oxford, he became close to John and Charles Wesley and joined them in the Methodist movement. He was also a friend of Jonathan Edwards, who invited him to preach in his Northampton, Massachusetts church. He toured the American colonies, preaching to tens of thousands. His powerful speaking style captured his listeners, moving even his friend, Benjamin Franklin, to consider his cause.

Samuel Hopkins (1721-1803), born in Connecticut, was an understudy of Jonathan Edwards, a theologian, and an abolitionist. He was ordained in 1743 and served at the Congregational Church at Housatonic, Massachusetts until 1769, and in 1770 became a minister of First Congregational Church in Newport.

John Newton (1725-1807) was a former slave trader. In 1748 he was converted while driving a ship through a storm, but did not give up the slave trade until 1754. Ten years later, he was ordained by the Church of England. He wrote many hymns, including the famous "Amazing Grace." By 1788, Newton had joined the abolitionist cause by writing about his life as a slave trader and serving as a mentor for younger abolitionists like William Wilberforce.

Hannah More (1745-1833) was a British writer and educator. During the 1770s she wrote plays that were produced on stage. By the 1780s she focused on her Evangelical faith and became involved in many philanthropic movements, writing various tracts and books, as well as poems about the abolition of slavery. A close friend of William Wilberforce, she was an active member of the abolitionist Clapham Sect.

Phoebe Worrall Palmer (1807-1874) was raised in a Methodist church and married a Methodist physician named Walter C. Palmer. They both became active revivalists during the Second Great Awakening in America. She was an evangelist and a leader in the holiness movement. Palmer led women's prayer meetings, helped the poor, cared for prisoners, and wrote tracts, articles, and books, including the famous *The Way to Holiness* (1845). She is often considered the forerunner of modern Pentecostalism.

Charles Grandison Finney (1792-1875) was a lawyer turned revivalist in America during the Second Great Awakening. Finney practiced law in New York, where his interest in Mosaic Law drew him to the Bible. He was licensed by Presbyterians as an evangelist, and later became a Congregationalist. Finney used techniques he called "new measures" to spread revival. One of these was the practice of the "anxious bench," a seat placed in the front of a church where sinners could recount their sins, much like a lawyer questions a witness in a courtroom. For his "new measures" he received severe condemnation from other Evangelicals, such as Lyman Beecher. Finney left New York for Ohio and joined Oberlin College as professor of theology and later became the school's president. He was also a minister at Oberlin's First Congregational Church.

Anthony Ashley Cooper (1801-1885), the 7th Earl of Shaftesbury, was a dedicated Evangelical social reformer and the president of the Foreign Bible Society. He was a member of the House of Commons from 1826. He secured reforms related to industry, such as shortening work days in the textile mills to 10 hours and promoting low-cost housing for urban workers. In 1842, he passed an act keeping women and children under 10 years old from working in the underground coal mines. He also passed the *Lunacy Act* of 1845, which forced British society to treat mentally ill people as human beings of unsound mind instead of as social outcasts to be locked away.

James Hudson Taylor (1832-1905) was one of the world's most successful missionaries. Because of his medical training, he was able to enter China, which was then closed to Christian missionaries. Leaving for China in 1853, Taylor's first missionary efforts were foiled by the folding of the missionary agency that sent him. As a result, he formed China Inland Mission in 1865 (which later became Overseas Missionary Fellowship). In 1866, Taylor, his wife Maria, and their children, along with a contingent of other missionaries, returned to China. Taylor drew criticism from other Protestant missionaries because he insisted on wearing the clothing of the Chinese people and preaching in Chinese. But Taylor was soon considered a model for international missions.

THE BEGINNINGS OF A MODERN WORLD

THE CLOSE OF the Great Awakening period saw a new world. It was a world where information traveled much faster, where foreign lands had become less mysterious, and where individuals began to understand themselves as one in a global population of billions. This changing relationship to the world created new opportunities for the gospel as well as new challenges.

THE INDUSTRIAL REVOLUTION

The *Industrial Revolution* began around 1760 in England. The primary workplace moved from the family farm to the factory, with a new division of labor. The discovery of new metals, and inventions like the steam engine, led to machines replacing humans and animals in production plants. These innovations increased production and made products that were once scarce now available to the common person. But they also created longer work hours and unhealthy working conditions. Families that used to work together on the farm now had separate occupations. Many families moved into overcrowded tenements, where disease spread more rapidly. Where churches had been a part of rural life, they were not part of factory life. So Christians, especially Methodists, quickly founded new ministries to reach those who faced different situations.

GOD VS. SCIENCE?

For most of the world's history, the *supernatural worldview* was a way of life. People did not question the existence of God and the spirit world. But that changed as new scientific principles were discovered.

Sir Isaac Newton (1642-1727), an English physicist and mathematician, published *Mathematical Principles of Natural Philosophy* in 1687. His work established what is now understood as the *mechanical universe*, or a universe that runs by forces or laws. Newton's ideas gave scientists the confidence that this world can be tested and certainties can be discovered. Newton understood gravity as something caused by God, but later generations of scientists wondered: if the universe consists of laws of nature, is God necessary? For the first time, scientists were willing to consider a universe without God.

The science of biology was turned upside down when Charles Darwin (1809-1882) published *On the Origin of Species* in 1859, proposing the theory of evolution. He concluded that the evolution of all life is guided by a process called *natural selection* in which those species that survive, do so because they have some advantage others don't have. When they pass on these traits to their children, species change over time. Perhaps some species even share common ancestors, Darwin said. Right away, theologians saw this as a direct challenge to the biblical account of creation and the historical reality of Adam and Eve. Charles Hodge (1797-1878), a professor at Princeton Theological Seminary, saw evolution as incompatible with Christianity. But his student, B.B. Warfield, also a professor at Princeton, remained open to the idea of an evolution that was directed by God. Christians have carried on this debate to the present day.

CHALLENGES TO BIBLICAL AUTHORITY

Other challenges to Christianity arose as philosophers and theologians discussed the nature of religion. Some said Christianity was simply the best of all human religions, but not the final or only one. They believed there was room for improvement in religion, leading to the development of religious ideas that focused almost entirely upon human beings, rather than God. Also, some biblical scholars began to question the reliability of the biblical text. When they began to notice similarities between the Bible and ancient texts of other religions, some concluded that the Bible is merely a human book and that Christianity was just a development of early primitive religions instead of the true gospel of Christ.

With so many challenges to the Bible and the work of the church, Christians of the Great Awakenings had their work cut out for them. They called people to return to the Bible as God's Word. They renewed the idea of a personal faith that expresses itself in loving action. But they also had to consider how the Bible relates to science, and they had to learn new ways to communicate their eternal faith to the changing modern world. Because the twentieth century was just around the corner.

Author Information

Mindy and Brandon Withrow are writers and active bloggers who have lived most recently in Philadelphia, Pennsylvania and Birmingham, Alabama. Brandon is adjunct professor of church history at Beeson Divinity School. They are both graduates of the Moody Bible Institute in Chicago; Brandon is also a graduate of Trinity Evangelical Divinity School and has a PhD in Historical Theology from Westminster Theological Seminary. One of their favorite activities is reading to their nieces and nephews.

Where We Got Our Information
and Other Helpful Resources

Barnett, Suzanne Wilson and John King Fairbank, eds. *Christianity in China*. Harvard University Asia Center, 1985.

Bowker, John. *World Religions: The Great Faiths Explored and Explained*. Dorling Kindersley, 1997.

Carey, Eustace. *Memoir of William Carey*. D.D. Jackson and Walford, 1836.

Corder, Susanna. *The Life of Elizabeth Fry, compiled from her Journal*. Henry Longstreth, 1855.

Encyclopedia Britannica 2007. Encyclopedia Britannica Online School Edition.

Fiske, D.T. *Faith Working by Love: As Exemplified in The Life of Fidelia Fiske*. Congregational Sabbath School and Publishing Society, 1868.

Hattersley, Roy. *The Life of John Wesley: A Brand from the Burning*. Doubleday, 2003.

Judson, Edward. *Adoniram Judson: His Life and Labors*. Hodder and Stoughton, 1883.

Larsen, Timothy, editor. *Biographical Dictionary of Evangelicals*. Inter-Varsity, 2003.

Livingstone, David. *Dr. Livingstone's Cambridge Lectures*. Cambridge University, 1860.

Livingstone, David. *Missionary Travels and Researches in South Africa*. Harper and Brothers, 1870.

Marsden, George M. *Jonathan Edwards: A Life*. Yale University Press, 2003.

Medhurst, W.H. *China: Its State and Prospects with Especial Reference to the Spread of the Gospel*. John Snow, 1818.

Metaxas, Eric. *Amazing Grace: William Wilberforce and the Heroic Campaign to End Slavery.* Harper, 2007.

Painter, Nell Irvin. *Sojourner Truth: A Life, A Symbol.* W. W. Norton, 1996.

Pal, Krishna. *The First Hindoo Convert: A Memoir of Krishna Pal.* American Baptist Publication Society, 1852.

Pease, Paul. *Travel with William Carey.* Day One Publications, 2005.

Philip, Robert. *The Life and Opinions of the Rev. William Milne.* John Snow, 1840.

Robert, Dana Lee. *American Women in Mission: A Social History of Their Thought and Practice.* Mercer University Press, 1997.

Rose, June. *Elizabeth Fry.* St. Martin's Press, 1980.

Seebohm, Benjamin. *Memoirs of the Life and Gospel Labours of Stephen Grellet, in Two Volumes.* Henry Longstreth, 1860.

Spickard, Paul R. and Kevin M. Cragg. *God's Peoples: A Social History of Christians.* Baker, 1994.

Stowe, Harriet Beecher. "Sojourner Truth, The Libyan Sibyl." *Atlantic Monthly.* April 1863.

Sweeney, Douglas A. *The American Evangelical Story: A History of the Movement.* Baker Academic, 2005.

Wilberforce, Robert Isaac and Samuel Wilberforce. *The Correspondence of William Wilberforce in Two Volumes.* J. Murray, 1840.

Wilberforce, Robert Isaac and Samuel Wilberforce. *The Life of William Wilberforce in Five Volumes.* J. Murray, 1838.

Wilberforce, William. "On the Horrors of the Slave Trade." In *The World's Greatest Orations, Vol. IV*, William Jennings Bryan, ed. Funk and Wagnalls, 1906.

Wolff, Christoph. *Johann Sebastian Bach: The Learned Musician.* W. W. Norton, 2000.

Woodbridge, John D., editor. *Ambassadors for Christ.* Moody Press, 1994.

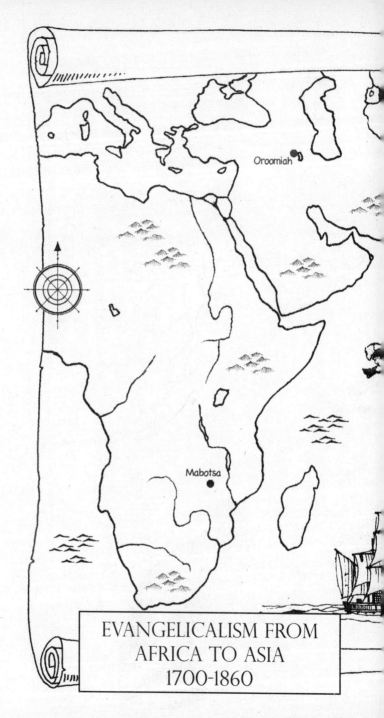

Oroomiah

Mabotsa

EVANGELICALISM FROM
AFRICA TO ASIA
1700-1860

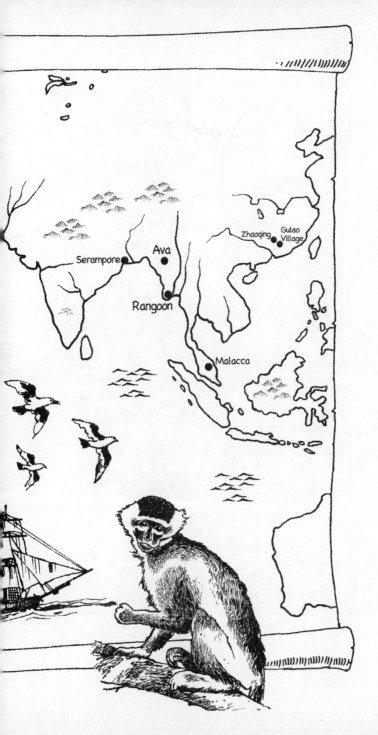

Serampore

Ava

Rangoon

Zhaoqing

Gulao
Village

Malacca

Liverpool

Cambridge ●

London ●

Paris ●

Leipzig

EVANGELICALISM IN
EUROPE 1700-1860

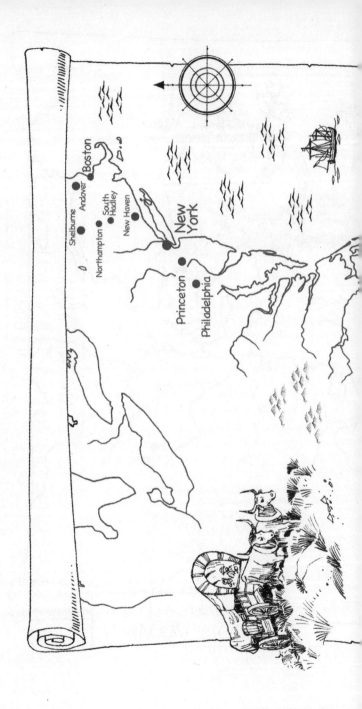

Boston

Shelburne

Andover

Northampton

South
Hadley

New Haven

New
York

Princeton

Philadelphia

Savannah

EVANGELICALISM IN
NORTHEASTERN AMERICA
1700-1860

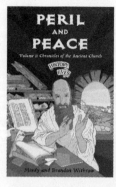

Peril and Peace,
Chronicles of the Ancient Church
History Lives, Volume 1
ISBN: 978-184550-082-5

Read the stories of Paul, Polycarp, Justin, Origen, Cyprian, Constantine, Athanasius, Ambrose, Augustine, John Chrysostom, Jerome, Patrick, and Benedict. People from the early and ancient church and discover the roots of Christianity. In their lives you will see the young and developing church struggling and growing in a hostile and difficult world. Watch in amazement as a varied selection of people from different countries, cultures and times merge together to form the Christian church. Learn from their mistakes and errors but more importantly learn from their amazing strengths and gifts. Marvel at the incredible things accomplished by God in such a short space of time.

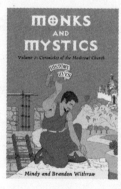

Monks and Mystics,
Chronicles of the Medieval Church
History Lives, Volume 2
ISBN: 978-1-84550-083-2

Read the stories of Gregory the Great, Boniface, Charlemagne, Constantine Methodius, Vladimir, Anselm of Canterbury, Bernard of Clairvaux, Francis of Assisi, Thomas Aquinas, Catherine of Sienna, John Wyclif and John Hus. You can discover how the young Christian church moved on into another era of time to face the crusades and the spread of Islam as well as the beginnings of universities and the Reformation. Learn from their mistakes and errors but more importantly learn from their amazing strengths and gifts. Marvel at God's wonderful care of his people - the church - the Christian church.

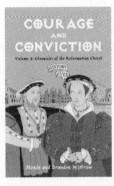

Courage and Conviction,
Chronicles of the Reformation Church
History Lives, Volume 3
ISBN: 978-1-84550-222-5

Read the stories of the reformers in the 16th and 17th centuries who changed the face of the Christian church forever. Meet the German monk, the French scholar, and the Scottish tutor who protested corruption in the church. Get to know the queens and explorers who risked everything for the freedom to worship according to their consciences. It was a time of war and upheaval, but also a time of promise and hope. From Erasmus and Luther to Katherine Parr and William Bradford, God used different personalities in different places to bring sweeping changes to church government and the way we worship. Learn from their mistakes and be encouraged by their amazing strengths and gifts.

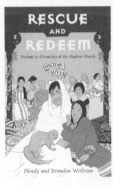

Rescue and Redeem,
Chronicles of the Modern Church
History Lives, Volume 5
ISBN: 978-1-84550-433-5

Read the stories of the Japanese samurai who traded his sword for a Bible and the Hawaiian princess whose faith strengthened her to defend her nation. Discover the German and Ugandan pastors who stood up to murderous dictators. Get to know the teacher in India who rescued child widows and the writer in Britain who created a world in a wardrobe. From Niijima Jo and Pandita Ramabai to Dietrich Bonhoeffer and Janani Luwum, they set out to rescue God's global people and redeem them to new life in Christ. Extra features throughout this book look deeper into issues such as modern Bible translation, living the Golden Rule, new developments in missions, and big moments in modern Christianity.